crocheted home

35 BEAUTIFUL DESIGNS FOR THROWS, CUSHIONS, BLANKETS AND MORE

kate eastwood

CICO BOOKS
LONDON NEW YORK

For my Dad,
Richard George Askew.

"How lucky I am to have something that makes
saying goodbye so hard.

Winnie the Pooh

Published in 2020 by CICO Books
An imprint of Ryland Peters & Small Ltd
20–21 Jockey's Fields, London WC1R 4BW
341 E 116th St New York, NY 10029

www.rylandpeters.com

10 9 8 7 6 5 4 3 2 1

Text © Kate Eastwood 2020

Design, illustration and photography © CICO
Books 2020

A CIP catalogue record for this book is
available from the British Library.

ISBN: 978-1-78249-894-0

Printed in China

Editor: Marie Clayton
Photographer: James Gardiner
Stylist: Nel Haynes
Illustrator: Stephen Dew

Junior Editor: Martha Gavin
Art director: Sally Powell
Production controller: Mai-Ling Collyer
Head of production: Patricia Harrington
Publishing manager: Penny Craig
Publisher: Cindy Richards

CONTENTS

Introduction 6

INTRODUCTION

Welcome to my crocheted home! I hope you enjoy your wander through, discovering all the different crocheted items made for each room and I very much hope they inspire you to fill your home with beautiful crochet creations too.

One of the things that I have loved the most since learning how to crochet has been the huge satisfaction gained in making things for my home and throughout this book I have been able to share many of my ideas with you. The changing times of year have played a huge part in my inspiration for many of the patterns as I love to change things around in my house with the seasons. From warm cosy blankets to seasonal cushions, and from useful storage baskets for spring cleaning and sorting, to Christmas decorations and table settings, there is something for everyone and for every room.

A lot of the crochet items I make are given as gifts to family and friends, from baby blankets for new-borns, to cushions for a new home or blankets to be taken to college, and I hope the patterns within this book will enable you to put together your own personalised gifts for those you love.

All the patterns have been given a skill rating so that, whatever your level of crochet, you will be able to work your way through them in your own time. Why not start with some of the simpler, quicker projects such as the Circular Table Mats (page 92), Tea Towel Edgings (page 90) or Hanger Covers (page 42) and work up to a longer, more detailed project such as the Striped Bolster Cushion (page 64) or the Striped Ruffle Blanket (page 44).

If I had to choose any favourite designs from this book it would have to be the Christmas and Easter decorations – I fell in love with these makes. The Spring Table Runner (page 102), made in eyelash yarn, was such fun to do and the little matching placemats can be hooked in minutes. The Christmas decorations will certainly be ones that are brought out each year in our house and I am already planning what little gifts to tuck into the tiny buckets and stockings on the Nordic Christmas Stocking String (page 111).

It has been an amazing few months coming up with the designs and making all 35 of the projects for this book and I hope they bring you as much joy as they have given me during the creating process. I wish you many happy hours of crocheting and may your home, like mine, be full of all things crochet!

CHAPTER 1

NURSERY

CLOUD AND STAR BABY BLANKET

This baby blanket is the perfect size for covering little ones in their car seats or buggies and is lightweight but warm. It makes a wonderful gift for any new baby, with the colours being interchangeable to match chosen colour schemes.

SKILL LEVEL ● ●

YARN AND MATERIALS

Debbie Bliss Baby Cashmerino (55% wool, 33% acrylic, 12% cashmere, 125m/137yd per 50g/1¾oz ball) 5-ply (sport) weight yarn:
   6 balls of Duck Egg shade 026 (A)

James C Brett Glisten (97% cotton, 3% polyester, 210m/230yd per 100g/3½oz ball) DK (light worsted) weight yarn:
   1 ball of shade GS4 (B)

Approx. 1m (1yd) thin white ribbon

Small amount of 100% polyester toy stuffing

HOOKS AND EQUIPMENT

3.5mm (US size E/4) crochet hook

3mm (US size C/2–D/3) crochet hook

Yarn needle

Safety pins

Sewing needle and thread

Foam matting or towel for blocking

Blocking pins

FINISHED MEASUREMENTS

Width 50cm (19¾in), length 60cm (23¾in)

TENSION (GAUGE)

15 sts x 15 rows = 6.5cm x 6cm (2½in x 2⅜in) working double crochet, using a 3.5mm (US size E/4) crochet hook.

ABBREVIATIONS

See page 127.

Blanket

Using 3.5mm (US size E/4) hook and A, ch106.
Row 1: 1dc in second ch from hook, 1dc in each ch to end, turn. *105 sts.*
Row 2: Ch1 (does not count as st), 1dc in each of next 105 sts, turn.
Rep Row 2 until work measures 56cm (22in), ending with a RS row.
Do not fasten off, do not turn.

BORDER

Round 1: Work a second dc in last st of row (corner made), work 1dc in each row end down left hand side, 2dc in corner st, work 1dc in each st along bottom, 2dc in corner st, work 1dc in each row end up right hand side of blanket, 2dc in corner st, sl st in first st of last row of blanket to join.
Round 2: Ch1 (counts as 1dc throughout), 1dc in same st as ch (corner made), [1dc in each st to corner, 2dc in corner st] 3 times, 1dc in each st to end, sl st in beg st in top of ch-1 to join.
Fasten off A.
Round 3: Join B to any st of border round with a sl st, ch1, working in BLO, work 1dc in each st around blanket edge, working 2dc in each corner st, sl st in top of ch-1 to join.
Round 4: Ch1, *sl st in next st, miss 1 st, 4htr in next st, miss 1 st, sl st in next st; rep from * around blanket edge, sl st in top of ch-1 to join.
Fasten off.

Stars

(make 13)
Using 3mm (US size C/2–D/3) hook and B, make a magic ring.

Round 1: 5dc in ring, sl st in top of first dc to join *5 sts.*

Round 2: Ch1, [2dc in next st] 5 times, sl st in top of ch-1 to join. *10 sts.*

Round 3: *Ch4, sl st in second ch from hook, 1dc in next ch, 1htr in next ch, miss 1 st on central circle and sl st in next st; rep from * 4 times to make 5 points in total, sl st in base of first point to join.
Fasten off.

Clouds

(make 2)
Using 3mm (US size C/2–D/3) hook and B, ch4.

Row 1: 2dc in second ch from hook, 1dc in next ch, 2dc in last ch. *5 sts.*

Turn at end of this and every following row.

Row 2: Ch1 (does not count as st throughout), 2dc in first st, 1dc in each of next 3 sts, 2dc in last st. *7 sts.*

Row 3: Ch1, 2dc in first st, 1dc in each of next 6 sts. *8 sts.*

Row 4: Ch1, 1dc in each of next 7 sts, 2dc in last st. *9 sts.*

Row 5: Ch1, 2dc in first st, 1dc in each of next 7 sts, 2dc in last st. *11 sts.*

Row 6: Ch1, 1dc in each of next 10 sts, 2dc in last st. *12 sts.*

Rows 7–8: Ch1, 1dc in each of next 12 sts.

Row 9: Ch1, dc2tog, 1dc in each of next 10 sts. *11 sts.*

Row 10: Ch1, 1dc in each of next 10 sts, 2dc in last st. *12 sts.*

Row 11: Ch1, 2dc in first st, 1dc in each of next 11 sts. *13 sts.*

Row 12: Ch1, 1dc in each of next 12 sts, 2dc in last st. *14 sts.*

Row 13: Ch1, 2dc in first st, 1dc in each of next 13 sts. *15 sts.*

Row 14: Ch1, 1dc in each of next 14 sts, 2dc in last st. *16 sts.*

Row 15: Ch1, 2dc in first st, 1dc in each of next 15 sts. *17 sts.*

Row 16: Ch1, 1dc in each of next 16 sts, 2dc in last st. *18 sts.*

Rows 17–20: Ch1, 1dc in each of next 18 sts.

Row 21: Ch1, dc2tog, 1dc in each of next 16 sts. *17 sts.*

Row 22: Ch1, 1dc in each of next 15 sts, dc2tog. *16 sts.*

Row 23: Ch1, dc2tog, 1dc in each of next 14 sts. *15 sts.*

Row 24: Ch1, 1dc in each of next 13 sts, dc2tog. *14 sts.*

Row 25: Ch1, dc2tog, 1dc in each of next 12 sts. *13 sts.*

Row 26: Ch1, 1dc in each of next 12 sts, 2dc in last st. *14 sts.*

Row 27: Ch1, 2dc in first st, 1dc in each of next 13 sts. *15 sts.*

Row 28: Ch1, 1dc in each of next 14 sts, 2dc in last st. *16 sts.*

Row 29: Ch1, 2dc in first st, 1dc in each of next 15 sts. *17 sts.*

Rows 30–32: Ch1, 1dc in each of next 17 sts.

Row 33: Ch1, dc2tog, 1dc in each of next 15 sts. *16 sts.*

Row 34: Ch1, 1dc in each of next 14 sts, dc2tog. *15 sts.*

Row 35: Ch1, dc2tog, 1dc in each of next 13 sts. *14 sts.*

Row 36: Ch1, 1dc in each of next 12 sts, dc2tog. *13 sts.*

Row 37: Ch1, dc2tog, 1dc in each of next 11 sts. *12 sts.*

Row 38: Ch1, 1dc in each of next 10 sts, dc2tog. *11 sts.*

Row 39: Ch1, 2dc in first st, 1dc in each of next 8 sts, dc2tog. *11 sts.*

Row 40: Ch1, dc2tog, 1dc in each of next 7 sts, dc2tog. *9 sts.*

Row 41: Ch1, dc2tog, 1dc in each of next 5 sts, dc2tog. *7 sts.*

Row 42: Ch1, dc2tog, 1dc in each of next 3 sts, dc2tog. *5 sts.*

Row 43: Ch1, dc2tog, 1dc in next st, dc2tog. *3 sts.*

Fasten off.

Making up and finishing

To finish the clouds, with RS facing, using 3mm (US size C/2–D/3) hook, join B at any point around the edge and work 1dc in each st and row end around the cloud edge, sl st in first st to join.

Sew in ends. Lay the blanket on a flat surface, RS up. Place the clouds where you want them to be and hold them in place with safety pins. Cut seven small lengths of ribbon and tuck three of them under the bottom edge of one cloud, and four under the bottom edge of the second cloud. Stitch the cloud securely in place, making sure there are some stitches securing the ribbons. Before you finish sewing all the way around carefully insert a small amount of toy stuffing so the cloud has a softly raised appearance. Repeat to attach the other cloud.

Now position the hanging stars where you want them to be and tuck a ribbon from the clouds under each star. Pin in place with safety pins. Using a sewing needle and thread, stitch the stars securely in place, ensuring that the ribbon is attached securely too. Position and sew down the remaining stars as desired.

Block the blanket by pinning it to foam matting or a towel with blocking pins. Spray lightly with water and allow to air dry.

STAR CUSHION

This small rectangular shaped cushion is the perfect size to pop on a nursery chair or at the end of a child's bed. Made in cotton yarn and with an envelope style back it is easy to remove the cover when needed so that it can be washed. With a neutral background, the colour of the stars can be changed to match your décor.

SKILL LEVEL ●

YARN AND MATERIALS

Cascade Ultra Pima (100% cotton, 200m/219yd per 100g/3½oz ball) DK (light worsted) weight yarn:
  3 balls of Buff shade 3719 (A)
  1 ball of Veiled Rose shade 3840 (B)

40 x 30cm (16 x 12in) cushion pad

2 snap fasteners

HOOKS AND EQUIPMENT

4mm (US size G/6) crochet hook

3mm (US size C/2–D/3) crochet hook

Yarn needle

Pins

Safety pins

Piece of cardboard same size as cushion pad

Sewing needle and thread

FINISHED MEASUREMENTS

Cushion: width 40cm (16in), height 30cm (12in)
Stars: 5cm (2in) from point to point

TENSION (GAUGE)

15 sts x 15 rows = 7.5 x 6cm (3 x 2⅜in) working double crochet, using a 4mm (US size G/6) crochet hook.

ABBREVIATIONS

See page 127.

Cushion cover

Using 4mm (US size G/6) hook and A, ch81.
Row 1: 1dc in second ch from hook, 1dc in each ch to end, turn. *80 sts.*
Row 2: Ch1 (does not count as st), 1dc in each of next 80 sts, turn.
Rep Row 2 until work measures 69cm (27in), ending with a RS row. Do not fasten off, do not turn.

BORDER
Work a second dc in last st of row (corner made), work 1dc in each row end down left hand side, 2dc in corner st, work 1dc in each st along bottom edge, 2dc in corner st, work 1dc in each row end up right-hand side of cushion, 2dc in corner st, sl st in first st of last row of cushion to join.
Fasten off

Stars

(make 15)
Using 3mm (US size C/2–D/3) crochet hook and B, make a magic ring.
Round 1: 5dc into ring, sl st in top of first dc to join. *5 sts.*
Round 2: Ch1 (does not count as st throughout), [2dc in next st] 5 times, sl st in top of ch-1 to join. *10 sts.*
Round 3: Ch1, [1dc in next st, 2dc in next st] 5 times, sl st in top of ch-1 to join. *15 sts.*
Round 4: *Ch5, sl st in second ch from hook, 1dc in next ch, 1htr in next ch, 1tr in next ch, miss 2 sts on central circle and sl st in next st; rep from * 4 times to make 5 points in total, sl st in base of first point to join.
Fasten off.

TIP

Why not make a baby blanket to match the cushion using matching yarn and colours – the Flower Baby Blanket (see page 17) would work perfectly for this!

Making up and finishing

Sew in ends. Lay the cushion cover on a flat surface, RS down. Place the cushion pad in the middle, fold the bottom of the cover up and the top of the cover down so that the cushion pad is enclosed, and the two edges overlap. Pin across the join at the back of the cushion where the opening will be – this will hold the cover in place whilst you position and attach the stars to the front of the cushion.

Turn the cushion over so that the front of the cushion is facing you and position the stars where you want them to be. Hold in place with safety pins. Slide the cushion pad out. Slide a piece of cardboard inside to avoid the front and back of the cushion getting stitched together. Using a sewing needle and thread stitch the stars securely in place.

Carefully remove the cardboard so as not to lose the shape of the cushion and pin the sides of the cushion shut. To join the sides, with the RS of the cushion facing you, using 4mm (US size G/6) hook and A, work a dc seam down each side joining the front and back edges together. Fasten off.

With the RS of the cushion facing you re-join B at the start of the dc side seam row and work 1dc in each st of dc side seam, turn. Ch1, *sl st in next st, ch2, sl st in second ch, sl st in next st on cushion edge; rep from * along the edge of the cushion. Fasten off.
Repeat on the other side of the cushion.

Stitch the two snap fasteners into place so that the opening of the cushion is closed, and the fasteners are hidden underneath the overlapping flap. Using a sewing needle and thread, sew the remaining two stars onto the back of the cushion, directly above where the fasteners are.

FLOWER BABY BLANKET

There can be nothing more special than spending time making a baby blanket – and this simple but modern design makes the perfect, unique gift for any new arrival. Worked in 100% cotton yarn it is light yet warm, and fully washable. The blanket is worked in double crochet and the daisies are made separately and sewn on afterwards.

SKILL LEVEL ●

YARN AND MATERIALS

Cascade Ultra Pima (100% cotton, 200m/219yd per 100g/3½oz ball) DK (light worsted) weight yarn:
    4 balls of Veiled Rose shade 3840 (A)
    1 ball in each of:
    Yellow Rose shade 3743 (B)
    White shade 3728 (C)

HOOKS AND EQUIPMENT

4mm (US size G/6) crochet hook

3.5mm (US size E/4) crochet hook

Yarn needle

Safety pins

Sewing needle and thread

FINISHED MEASUREMENTS

Width 57cm (22½in), length 70cm (27½in)
One flower measures approx. 6cm (2⅜in) diameter

TENSION (GAUGE)

15 sts x 15 rows = 7.5 x 6.5cm (3 x 2½in) working double crochet, using a 4mm (US size G/6) crochet hook.

ABBREVIATIONS

See page 127.

Blanket

Using 4mm (US size G/6) hook and A, ch113.
Row 1: 1dc in second ch from hook, 1dc in each ch to end, turn. *112 sts.*
Row 2: Ch1 (does not count as st throughout), 1dc in each st to end, turn.
Rep Row 2 until work measures 64.5cm (25½in), ending with RS facing. Do not turn and do not fasten off A at end of last row.

BORDER

Round 1: Work a second dc in final st of prev row, then work 1dc in each row end down left-hand side, 2dc in corner st, 1dc in each st along bottom edge, 2dc in corner st, 1dc in each row end up right-hand side, sl st in top of first dc of prev row to join.
Fasten off A.
Round 2: With RS facing, join C at top right-hand corner of blanket, ch1, [1dc in each st to corner, 2dc in corner st] 4 times, sl st in top of ch-1 to join.
Round 3: *Ch2, sl st in each of next 2 sts; rep from * around edge of blanket.
Finish off.

Daisy

(make 13)

Using 3.5mm (US size E/4) hook and B, make a magic ring.

Round 1: 7dc into ring, sl st in top of first dc to join round. *7 sts.*

Round 2: Ch1 (does not count as st), 2dc in each st to end, sl st in top of first dc to join round. *14 sts.*
Fasten off B.

Round 3: Join C in any dc of central ring, *ch6, working back down ch, miss first ch, 1htr in each of next 5 ch, sl st in each of next 2 sts on central ring; rep from * 6 times to make 7 petals in total, sl st in base of first petal to join round.
Fasten off.

Making up and finishing

Sew in any ends. Lay the blanket RS up on a flat surface, and position the daisies where you want them to be. Pin the flowers in place with safety pins. Using a sewing needle and thread stitch the daisies securely onto the blanket.

SPOTTED TISSUE BOX COVER

Make the tissue boxes around your home a whole lot more interesting by crocheting this simple cover that will simply slip over the top of a regular-sized, rectangular box of tissues.

SKILL LEVEL ● ●

YARN AND MATERIALS:

Cascade Ultra Pima (100% cotton, 200m/219yd per 100g/3½oz ball) DK (light worsted) weight yarn:
  1 ball of Natural shade 3718 (A)

Patons Fairytale Cloud (100% polyester, 82m/90yd per 25g/⅞oz ball) DK (light worsted) weight yarn:
  1 ball of Camel shade 1010 (B)

1 box of tissues, length 22.5cm, width 11.5cm, height 7cm (9 x 4½ x 2¾in)

HOOKS AND EQUIPMENT

3.5mm (US size E/4) crochet hook

3mm (US size C/2–D/3) crochet hook

Yarn needle

Safety pins

Sewing needle and thread

FINISHED MEASUREMENTS

Length 23cm (9in), width 13cm (5¼in), height 8cm (3¼in)

TENSION (GAUGE)

15 sts x 15 rows = 7 x 6.5cm (2¾ x 2½in) working double crochet, using a 3.5mm (US size E/4) crochet hook and Cascade Ultra Pima.

ABBREVIATIONS

See page 127.

Box cover

TOP
Using 3.5mm (US size E/4) hook and A, ch44.
Row 1: 1dc in second ch from hook, 1dc in each ch to end, turn. *43 sts.*
Row 2: Ch1 (does not count as st throughout), 1dc in each st to end, turn.
Rows 3–14: Rep Row 2.
Row 15: Ch1, 1dc in each of first 14 sts, ch17, miss next 15 sts, 1dc in each of last 14 sts, turn.
Row 16: Ch1, 1dc in each of first 14 sts, miss first ch, 1dc in each of next 15 ch, miss last ch, 1dc in each of last 14 sts, turn. *43 sts.*
Row 17: Ch1, 1dc in each st to end, turn.
Rows 18–29: Rep Row 17.
At end of Row 29, do not turn, ch1, 1dc in each row end down short side, ch1, 1dc in each st across bottom edge, ch1, 1dc in each row end up other short side, ch1, 1dc in each st along top edge, ch1, sl st in first ch-1 to join. Fasten off.

LONG SIDES
Row 1: With RS facing join A in BLO of right-hand corner of one long side of top piece, 1ch (does not count as st throughout), 1dc BLO in same st, 1dc BLO in each of next 42 sts to end of long side, turn. *43 sts.*
Row 2: Ch1, 1dc in each st to end, turn.
Rows 3–17: Rep Row 2.
Fasten off.
Rep on opposite side of piece to make second long side.

SHORT SIDES

Row 1: With RS facing join A in BLO of right-hand corner of one short side of top piece, 1ch (does not count as st throughout), 1dc BLO in same st, 1dc BLO in each of next 29 sts to end of short side, turn. *30 sts.*
Row 2: Ch1, 1dc in each st to end, turn.
Rows 3–17: Rep Row 2.
Fasten off.
Rep on opposite side of piece to make second short side.

JOINING THE SIDES

With WS tog and starting at top each time, fold the sides down to make a box shape and work a dc seam down each corner.
Fasten off.

EDGING

Using 3.5mm (US size E/4) hook join C at one bottom corner, 1dc in each st around bottom edge, sl st in top of first dc to join.
Fasten off.
Using 3.5mm (US size E/4) hook join C at one top corner, work dc around top edge of box, working in FLO of each st from Row 1 where sides join top of box.
Fasten off.

Spots

(make 26)
Work in a continuous spiral.
Using 3mm (US size C/2–D/3) hook and B, make a magic ring.
Round 1: 5dc into ring. *5 sts.*
Round 2: 2dc in each st to end, sl st in top of first dc to join round. *10 sts.*
Fasten off.

Making up and finishing

Sew in ends.

Position the spots where you want them to be and fasten with safety pins. Using a sewing needle and thread, stitch the spots securely into place.

STARS AND BOBBLES BLANKET

Whether it's laid on top of a child's bed or left on the sofa for those lazy-day snuggles, this child's blanket will be much loved by any little one. Made in the colours of your choice this can be personalised to suit and will offer warm cuddles whenever needed.

SKILL LEVEL ● ●

YARN AND MATERIALS

Lion Brand Touch of Alpaca (90% acrylic, 10% alpaca, 189m/207yd per 100g/3½oz ball) aran (worsted) weight yarn:
   8 balls of Blush shade 104 (A)
   2 balls of Taupe shade 123 (B)

HOOKS AND EQUIPMENT

5.5mm (US size I/9) crochet hook

Yarn needle

Sewing needle and thread

Stitch marker

Safety pins

Foam matting or towel for blocking

Blocking pins

FINISHED MEASUREMENTS

Blanket: width 80cm (31½in), length 125cm (49in)
Stars: 10cm (4in) from point to point

TENSION (GAUGE)

15 sts x 15 rows = 9 x 8cm (3½ x 3⅛in) working double crochet, using a 5.5mm (US size I/9) crochet hook.

ABBREVIATIONS

See page 127.

SPECIAL ABBREVIATION

MB (make bobble): [yarn round hook, insert hook in stitch, yarn round hook, pull yarn through work, yarn round hook, pull yarn through first 2 loops on hook] 6 times all in same stitch, yarn round hook, pull through all loops on hook

Blanket

Using A, ch113.
Row 1: 1dc in second ch from hook, 1dc in each ch to end, turn. *112 sts.*
Row 2: Ch1 (does not count as st), 1dc in each st to end, turn.
Rep Row 2 until work measures 105cm (41½in), ending with a RS row. Do not fasten off, do not turn.

BORDER

Round 1: Work a second dc in last st of row (corner made), work 1dc in each row end down left-hand side, 2dc in corner st, work 1dc in each st along bottom edge, 2dc in corner st, work 1dc in each row end up right-hand side of blanket, 2dc in corner st, sl st in first st of last row of blanket to join.
Round 2: Ch1 (counts as 1dc throughout), 1dc in same st as ch (corner made), [1dc in each st to corner, 2dc in corner st] 3 times, 1dc in each st to end, sl st in top of ch-1 to join at end of round.
Do not fasten off A, leave it at back of work, join in B.
Rounds 3–4: Using B, rep Round 2.
Rounds 5–9: Using A, rep Round 2.

Tip

In the bobble round you will be working the dc in A and the bobbles in B. Lay the yarn not in use across the top of the work, working over it to conceal it as you go.

Round 10 (Bobble Round): Using A, ch1, 1dc in same st as ch (corner made), 1dc in each of next 5 dc, using B, MB in next st, using A, 1dc in each of next 12 dc (working over B to conceal it), using B, MB in next st. Cont around, working 12dc in A between each bobble with bobbles in B, and working 2dc in each corner st of round – as you approach each corner you may need to adapt number of dc between last couple of bobbles so they are evenly spaced – sl st in top of ch-1 to join at end of round. Fasten off B.
Rounds 11–15: Using A, rep round 2.
Fasten off A.
Rounds 16–17: Using B, rep round 2.
Round 18: Ch1, *working in BLO throughout, sl st in next st, ch2, sl st in first ch, sl st in next st; rep from * around edge of blanket, sl st in top of ch-1 to join at end of round. Fasten off.

Stars

(make 13)
Using B make a magic ring.
Round 1: 5dc into ring. *5 sts.*
Work in a continuous spiral. PM in last st and move up as each round is finished.
Round 2: 2dc in each st to end. *10 sts.*
Round 3: [1dc in next st, 2dc in next st] 5 times. *15 sts.*
Round 4: [1dc in each of next 2 sts, 2dc in next st] 5 times, sl st in top of first dc to join. *20 sts.*

MAKE POINTS
Round 5: *Ch7, sl st in second ch from hook, 1dc in next ch, 1htr in next ch, 1tr in next ch, 1dtr in next ch, 1tr in last ch, miss 3 sts on central circle and sl st in next st; rep from * 4 times to make 5 points in total, sl st in base of first point to join.
Fasten off.

Making up and finishing

Sew in ends. Lay the blanket on a flat surface. Position the stars where you want them to be and hold them in place with safety pins. Using a sewing needle and thread stitch the stars securely in place. Block the blanket by pinning it on to foam matting or a towel with blocking pins. Spray lightly with water and allow to air dry.

SPOTTY POMPOM CUSHION

With spots and pompoms galore, this cushion will add a wonderful contemporary touch to any home. The cover has a simple overlap opening at the back so that it can be removed for washing.

SKILL LEVEL ●

YARN AND MATERIALS

Cascade Ultra Pima (100% cotton, 200m/219yd per 100g/3½oz ball) DK (light worsted) weight yarn:
 4 balls of Natural shade 3718 (A)

Patons Fairytale Cloud (100% polyester, 82m/90yd per 25g/⅞oz ball) DK (light worsted) weight yarn:
 1 ball of Grey shade 1090 (B)

2m (2¼yd) grey pompom edging

40 x 40cm (16 x 16in) cushion pad

3 snap fasteners

3 decorative buttons

HOOKS AND EQUIPMENT

4mm (US size G/6) crochet hook

3mm (US size C/2–D/3) crochet hook

Yarn needle

Safety pins

Sewing needle and thread

FINISHED MEASUREMENTS

46cm (18¼in) x 46cm (18¼in)

TENSION (GAUGE)

15 sts x 15 rows = 7.5 x 7cm (3 x 2¾in) working double crochet, using a 4mm (US size G/6) crochet hook and Cascade Ultra Pima.

ABBREVIATIONS

See page 127.

Cushion cover front panel

Using 4mm (US size G/6) hook and A, ch81.
Row 1: 1dc in second ch from hook, 1dc in each ch to end, turn. *80 sts.*
Row 2: Ch1 (does not count as st throughout), 1dc in each st to end, turn.
Rep Row 2 until work measures 39.5cm (15½in), ending with RS facing, do not turn.

EDGING

Round 1: Work a second dc in final st of prev row, then work 1dc in each row end down left-hand side, 2dc in corner st, 1dc in each st along bottom edge, 2dc in corner st, 1dc in each row end up right-hand side, 1dc in same st as first dc of prev row, sl st in top of first dc of prev row to join round.
Fasten off.
Round 2: With RS facing, join B at top right-hand corner of panel, ch1, [1dc in each st to corner, 2dc in corner st] 4 times, sl st in top of ch-1 to join round.
Fasten off.

Upper back panel

Using 4mm (US size G/6) hook and A, ch81.
Row 1: 1dc in second ch from hook, 1dc in each ch to end, turn. *80 sts.*
Row 2: Ch1 (does not count as st), 1dc in each st to end, turn.
Rep Row 2 until work measures 21cm (8¼in), ending with RS facing, do not turn.

Spots

(make 19)
Work in a continuous spiral.
Using 3mm (US size C/2–D/3) hook and B, make a magic ring.
Round 1: 8dc into ring. *8 sts.*
Round 2: 2dc in each st to end, sl st in top of first dc to join round. *16 sts.*
Fasten off.

Making up and finishing

Place the front cover RS down with the pompom edging around all four sides, making sure the pompoms hang over the edge. Add two back panels WS down on top, with outer edges aligned so they overlap in the centre. Pin all the layers in place with safety pins. Using a sewing needle and thread, stitch the sides together all the way around the cushion, making sure the pompom edging is stitched in too.

Put the cushion pad into the cover and pin across the join at the back to hold the cover in place whilst you position and attach the spots to the front of the cushion. Turn the cushion over so that front is facing you and position the spots where you want them to be. Hold them in place with safety pins, then slide the cushion pad out. Using a sewing needle and thread, stitch the spots securely in place being careful not to stitch right through to the back layers of the cover.

Place the cushion pad back inside and stitch the three snap fasteners evenly spaced along the inside of the overlap to close the cover. Using a sewing needle and thread, sew the three buttons onto the back of the cushion, directly above the snap fasteners.

EDGING

Round 1: Work a second dc in final st of prev row, then work 1dc in each row end down left-hand side, 2dc in corner st, 1dc in each st along bottom edge, 2dc in corner st, 1dc in each row end up right-hand side, 1dc in same st as first dc of prev row, sl st in top of first dc of prev row to join round.
Fasten off.

Lower back panel

Using 4mm (US size G/6) hook and A, ch81.
Row 1: 1dc in second ch from hook, 1dc in each ch to end, turn. *80 sts.*
Row 2: Ch1 (does not count as st), 1dc in each st to end, turn.
Rep Row 2 until work measures 24cm (9½in), ending with RS facing, do not turn.

EDGING

Round 1: Work a second dc in final st of prev row, then work 1dc in each row end down left-hand side, 2dc in corner st, 1dc in each st along bottom edge, 2dc in corner st, 1dc in each row end up right-hand side, 1dc in same st as first dc of prev row, sl st in top of first dc of prev row to join round.
Fasten off.

> ## Tip
>
> To prevent you accidentally sewing the front of the cushion to the back when sewing on the spots, slide a piece of cardboard inside the cover.

BALLOON CUSHION

Add this bright balloon cushion to any nursery or child's room for an instant burst of colour. With the ribbon strings on the balloons and a colourful pompom edge, there are also textures galore for little fingers to explore.

SKILL LEVEL ● ●

YARN AND MATERIALS

DMC Natura Just Cotton Medium (100% cotton, 75m/82yd per 50g/1¾oz ball) aran (worsted) weight yarn:
  8 balls of shade 03 (A)

Drops Cotton Merino (50% cotton, 50% wool, 110m/121yd per 50g/1¾oz ball) DK (light worsted) weight yarn:
  1 ball each of:
  Sea Green shade 29 (B)
  Cerise shade 14 (C)
  Pistachio shade 10 (D)

40 x 40cm (16 x 16in) cushion pad

Small amount of 100% polyester toy stuffing

50cm (20in) each of ribbon in 3 colours to match balloons

1m (1yd) of pompom edging

3 snap fasteners

3 buttons

HOOKS AND EQUIPMENT

5mm (US size H/8) crochet hook

3.5mm (US size E/4) crochet hook

Yarn needle

Pins

Safety pins

Piece of cardboard same size as cushion pad

Sewing needle and thread

FINISHED MEASUREMENTS

Width 42cm (16½in), length 42cm (16½in)

TENSION (GAUGE)

15 sts x 15 rows = 10 x 9cm (4 x 3½in) working double crochet, using a 5mm (US size H/8) crochet hook and DMC Natura Just Cotton Medium.

ABBREVIATIONS

See page 127.

Cushion cover

Using 5mm (US size H/8) hook and A, ch61.
Row 1: 1dc in second ch from hook, 1dc in each ch to end, turn. *60 sts.*
Row 2: Ch1 (does not count as st throughout), 1dc in each of next 60 sts, turn.
Rep Row 2 until work measures 85cm (33½in), ending with a RS row.
Do not fasten off.

BORDER
Round 1: Work a second dc in last st of prev row (corner made), work 1dc in each row end down left-hand side, 2dc in corner st, work 1dc in each st along bottom edge, 2dc in corner st, work 1dc in each row end up right-hand side, 2dc in corner st, sl st in first st of last row of cushion to join.
Fasten off A.

EDGES

With RS of cover facing you, join C at top of one long edge with a sl st, ch1 and work 1dc in each st along edge. Rep on other long edge.
Fasten off.

Balloons

(make 1 each in B, C and D)
Using 3.5mm (US size E/4) hook and either B, C or D, ch10.
Row 1: 1dc in second ch from hook, 1dc in each ch to end. *9 sts.*
Turn at end of this row and every foll row.
Row 2: Ch1 (does not count as st throughout), dc2tog, 1dc in each of next 5 dc, dc2tog. *7 sts.*
Row 3: Ch1, dc2tog, 1dc in each of next 3 dc, dc2tog. *5 sts.*
Row 4: Ch1, dc2tog, 1dc in next st, dc2tog. *3 sts.*
Row 5: Ch1, [2dc in next st] 3 times. *6 sts.*
Row 6: Ch1, 2dc in next st, 1dc in each of next 4 dc, 2dc in last st. *8 sts.*
Row 7: Ch1, 2dc in next st, 1dc in each of next 6 dc, 2dc in last st. *10 sts.*
Row 8: Ch1, 2dc in next st, 1dc in each of next 8 dc, 2dc in last st. *12 sts.*
Row 9: Ch1, 2dc in next st, 1dc in each of next 10 dc, 2dc in last st. *14 sts.*
Row 10: Ch1, 2dc in next st, 1dc in each of next 12 dc, 2dc in last st. *16 sts.*
Rows 11–12: Ch1, 1dc in each st to end.
Row 13: Ch1, 2dc in next st, 1dc in each of next 14 dc, 2dc in last st. *18 sts.*
Row 14: Ch1, 1dc in each st to end.
Row 15: Ch1, 2dc in next st, 1dc in each of next 16 dc, 2dc in last st. *20 sts.*
Rows 16–23: Ch1, 1dc in each st to end.
Row 24: Ch1, dc2tog, 1dc in each of next 16 dc, dc2tog. *18 sts.*
Row 25: Ch1, dc2tog, 1dc in each of next 14 dc, dc2tog. *16 sts.*
Row 26: Ch1, dc2tog, 1dc in each of next 12 dc, dc2tog. *14 sts.*

Row 27: Ch1, dc2tog, 1dc in each of next 10 dc, dc2tog. *12 sts.*
Row 28: Ch1, dc2tog, 1dc in each of next 8 dc, dc2tog. *10 sts.*
Row 29: Ch1, dc2tog, 1dc in each of next 6 dc, dc2tog. *8 sts.*
Row 30: Ch1, dc2tog, 1dc in each of next 4 dc, dc2tog. *6 sts.*
Row 31: Ch1, [dc2tog] 3 times. *3 sts.*
Fasten off.
With RS facing, re-join yarn at any point on edge of balloon with a sl st, ch1 and work dc evenly around edge of balloon, sl st in top of ch-1 to join.
Fasten off.

Making up and finishing

Sew in ends. Lay the cushion cover on a flat surface, RS down. Place the cushion pad in the middle, fold the bottom of the cover up and the top of the cover down so that the cushion pad is enclosed, and the two edges overlap. Pin across the join at the back of the cushion where the opening will be. This will hold the cover in place whilst you position and attach the balloons to the front of the cushion.

Turn the cushion over so that the RS is facing you and position the balloons where you want them to be. Hold in place with safety pins. Slide the cushion pad out. Slide a piece of cardboard inside to avoid the front and back of the cushion getting stitched together. Using a sewing needle and thread stitch the balloons securely in place, leaving a small gap at the centre bottom of each balloon and adding a small amount of toy stuffing into the balloon as you stitch to give a slightly raised appearance.

Now stitch the ribbons in position for the balloon strings, tucking the ribbon end underneath the bottom of the balloon and stitching the remaining gap closed. Add a small matching bow to each balloon.

Carefully remove the cardboard so as not to lose the shape of the cushion. Cut the piece of pompom edging in half and place a piece on each side of the cushion so that the pompom tape is enclosed between the front and back of the cushion. Pin the sides of the cushion shut so that the front of the cushion, the pompom edging, and the back of the cushion are all held in place. Use a sewing needle and thread to stitch the sides of the cushion securely together.

Stitch the three snap fasteners into place so that the opening of the cushion is closed, and the fasteners are hidden underneath the overlapping flap. Using a sewing needle and thread, sew the three buttons onto the back of the cushion, directly above where the fasteners are.

CHAPTER 2

BEDROOM & BATHROOM

BOBBLY BATHMAT

Made in cotton jersey yarn, this bathmat is beautifully chunky but soft underfoot as well. The mat is worked with two strands of yarn and a large hook, making it a quick and easy project.

SKILL LEVEL ● ●

YARN AND MATERIALS

Katia Big Ribbon (50% cotton, 50% polyester, 72m/79yd per 200g/7oz ball) super chunky (super bulky) weight yarn:
  2 balls of shade 3 (A)
  2 balls of shade 10 (B)

DMC Natura XL (100% cotton, 75m/82yd per 100g/3½oz ball) super chunky (super bulky) weight yarn:
  2 balls of shade 41 (C)

HOOKS AND EQUIPMENT

8mm (US size L/11) crochet hook

7mm (US size K10½–L/11) crochet hook

Yarn needle

FINISHED MEASUREMENTS

Width 68cm (26¾in), length 40cm (16in)

TENSION (GAUGE)

5 sts x 5 rows = 8 x 8cm (3¼ x 3¼in) working double crochet, using an 8mm (US size L/11) crochet hook with 1 strand of A and 1 strand of B held tog.

ABBREVIATIONS

See page 127.

SPECIAL ABBREVIATION

MB loop (make bobble loop): [yarn round hook, insert hook in st, yarn round hook, pull through st as if starting a htr, pull loop up to htr height] 5 times all in the same st, leaving all loops on hook, yarn round hook and pull through all loops on hook, ch1.

Bathmat

Using 8mm (US size L/11) hook with 1 strand of A and 1 strand of B held tog, ch41.
Row 1: 1dc in second ch from hook, 1dc in each ch to end, turn. *40 sts.*
Row 2: Ch1 (does not count as a st throughout), 1dc in each of next 40 sts, turn.
Rows 3–24: Rep Row 2.
Fasten off.

BORDER
Round 1 (RS): Using 7mm (US size K10½–L/11) hook, join C with a sl st at any point on edge of bathmat, ch1, 2dc in same st, 2dc in each st and row end around edge of bathmat, sl st in top of beg ch-1 to join, turn work.
Round 2 (WS): Ch1, *sl st in each of next 2 sts, MB loop in next st; rep from * to end, sl st in top of ch-1 to join. Fasten off.

Making up and finishing

Ensure all yarn ends are sewn in securely.

TIP

You could work the border in an accent colour to go with your bathroom. Or, for a neutral colourway, match the bobbly border to the colour of the bathmat.

LIDDED BASKETS

For somewhere to store cotton wool, cosmetics, jewellery or loose change, these lidded baskets make the perfect addition to a bathroom or bedroom. Worked in neutral tones or bright colours, they can be made to match any décor. The baskets are worked with two strands of aran (worsted) weight yarn to give a good rigidity to the finished items.

SKILL LEVEL ● ●

YARN AND MATERIALS

DMC Natura Just Cotton Medium (100% cotton, 75m/82yd per 50g/1¾oz ball) aran (worsted) weight yarn:

For the small lidded basket
   1 ball of shade 31 (A)
   1 ball of shade 03 (B)

For the large striped lidded basket
   2 balls of shade 31 (A)
   2 balls of shade 03 (B)

Small amount of co-ordinating ribbon

HOOKS AND EQUIPMENT

4.5mm (US size 7) crochet hook

3.5mm (US size E/4) crochet hook

Yarn needle

Stitch marker

FINISHED MEASUREMENTS

Small basket: diameter 10cm (4in), height 7.5cm (3in)
Large striped basket: diameter 14.5cm (6in), height 11.5cm (4½in)

TENSION (GAUGE)

10 sts x 10 rounds = 8 x 7cm (3¼ x 2¾in) working double crochet, using a 4.5mm (US size 7) crochet hook with 2 strands of yarn held tog.

ABBREVIATIONS

See page 127.

Small basket

Using 4.5mm (US size 7) hook with 1 strand of A and 1 strand of B held tog, make a magic ring.
Round 1: 6dc in ring, sl st in top of first dc to join. *6 sts.*
Work in a continuous spiral. PM in last st and move up as each round is finished.
Round 2: [2dc in next st] 6 times. *12 sts.*
Round 3: [1dc in next st, 2dc in next st] 6 times. *18 sts.*
Round 4: 1dc in first st, 2dc in next st, [1dc in each of next 2 sts, 2dc in next st] 5 times, 1dc in last st. *24 sts.*
Round 5: [1dc in each of next 3 sts, 2dc in next st] 6 times. *30 sts.*
Round 6: 1dc in each of next 2 sts, 2dc in next st, [1dc in each of next 4 sts, 2dc in next st] 5 times, 1dc in each of last 2 sts. *36 sts.*
Round 7: Ch1 (does not count as st throughout), working in back loops only, 1dc in each st around, sl st in top of ch-1 to join. *36 sts.*
Beg working in joined rounds.
Rounds 8–15: Ch1, working into both loops as normal, 1dc in each st around, sl st in top of ch-1 to join.
Fasten off.

Small basket lid

Using 4.5mm (US size 7) hook with 1 strand of A and 1 strand of B held tog, make a magic ring.
Rounds 1–6: Work as Rounds 1–6 of small basket. *36 sts.*
Round 7: [1dc in each of next 5 sts, 2dc in next st] 6 times. *42 sts.*
Round 8: Ch1 (does not count as st throughout), working in back loops only, 1dc in each st around, sl st in top of ch-1 to join. *42 sts.*
Beg working in joined rounds.
Rounds 9–10: Ch1, working in both loops as normal, 1dc in each st around, sl st in top of ch-1 to join.
Fasten off.

Large striped basket

Using 4.5mm (US size 7) hook and 2 strands of A held tog, make a magic ring.

Round 1: 6dc in ring, sl st in top of first dc to join. *6 sts.* Work in a continuous spiral. PM in last st and move up as each round is finished.

Round 2: [2dc in each st] 6 times. *12 sts.*

Round 3: [1dc in next st, 2dc in next st] 6 times. *18 sts.*

Round 4: 1dc in first st, 2dc in next st, [1dc in each of next 2 sts, 2dc in next st] 5 times, 1dc in last st. *24 sts.*

Round 5: [1dc in each of next 3 sts, 2dc in next st] 6 times. *30 sts.*

Round 6: 1dc in each of next 2 sts, 2dc in next st, [1dc in each of next 4 sts, 2dc in next st] 5 times, 1dc in each of last 2 sts. *36 sts.*

Round 7: [1dc in each of next 5 sts, 2dc in next st] 6 times. *42 sts.*

Round 8: 1dc in each of next 3 sts, 2dc in next st, [1dc in each of next 6 sts, 2dc in next st] 5 times, 1dc in each of last 3 sts. *48 sts.*

Round 9: [1dc in each of next 7 sts, 2dc in next st] 6 times. *54 sts.*

Round 10: Ch1 (does not count as st throughout), working in back loops only, 1dc in each st around, sl st in top of ch-1 to join. *54 sts.*
Beg working in joined rounds.

Round 11: Ch1, working in both loops as normal, 1dc in each st around, sl st in top of ch-1 to join. Leave 2 strands of A at back of work.

Rounds 12–13: Using 2 strands of B held tog, ch1, 1dc in each st around, sl st in top of ch-1 to join at end of each round.

Rounds 14–15: Using 2 strands of A and leaving 2 strands of B at back of work, ch1, 1dc in each st around, sl st in top of ch-1 to join at end of each round. Cont working 2 rounds in each colour until you have 4 stripes in A and 3 stripes in B.
Fasten off.

Large striped basket lid

Using 4.5mm (US size 7) hook and 2 strands of B held tog, make a magic ring.

Round 1: 6dc in ring, sl st in top of first dc to join. *6 sts.*

Round 2: Ch1 (does not count as st throughout), [2dc in next st] 6 times, sl st in ch-1 to join. *12 sts.*

Round 3: Using 2 strands of A held tog and leaving both strands of B at back of work, ch1, [1dc in next st, 2dc in next st] 6 times, sl st in ch-1 to join. *18 sts.*

Round 4: Ch1, 1dc in first st, 2dc in next st, [1dc in each of next 2 sts, 2dc in next st] 5 times, 1dc in last st, sl st in ch-1 to join. *24 sts.*

Round 5: Using B and leaving A at back of work, ch1, [1dc in each of next 3 sts, 2dc in next st] 6 times, sl st in top of ch-1 to join. *30 sts.*

Round 6: Ch1, 1dc in each of next 2 sts, 2dc in next st, [1dc in each of next 4 sts, 2dc in next st] 5 times, 1dc in each of last 2 sts, sl st in top of ch-1 to join. *36 sts.*

Round 7: Using A and leaving B at back of work, ch1, [1dc in each of next 5 sts, 2dc in next st] 6 times, sl st in top of ch-1 to join. *42 sts.*

Round 8: Ch1, 1dc in each of next 3 sts, 2dc in next st, [1dc in each of next 6 sts, 2dc in next st] 5 times, 1dc in each of next 3 sts, sl st in top of ch-1 to join. *48 sts.*

Round 9: Using B and leaving A at back of work, ch1, [1dc in each of next 7 sts, 2dc in next st] 6 times, sl st in top of ch-1 to join. *54 sts.*

Round 10: Ch1, 1dc in each of next 4 sts, 2dc in next st, [1dc in each of next 8 sts, 2dc in next st] 5 times, 1dc in each of next 4 sts, sl st in top of ch-1 to join. *60 sts.*

Round 11: Ch1, working in back loops only, 1dc in each st around, sl st in top of ch-1 to join. *60 sts.*

Rounds 12–13: Using A and leaving B at back of work, ch1, working in both loops as normal, 1dc in each st around, sl st in top of ch-1 to join at end of each round.
Fasten off.

When working the joined rounds, finish each round by joining back to the beginning with a slip stitch. Chain 1 and work the first stitch from the next round in the double crochet at the base of the chain – this will give you a straight, neat join all the way up the side of the basket, and from the centre of the lid to the outer edge.

To give your basket extra strength you may find it helpful to cut out a cardboard disc to fit exactly into the base of each basket, and another for the lid.

Making up and finishing

FINISHING THE BASKET

Using 1 strand of either A or B and 3.5mm (US size E/4) hook, join yarn in any unworked front loop from Round 7 of small basket or Round 10 of large striped basket. Work crab stitch around the base of the basket as follows: continuing to work just in the unworked front loops and working clockwise with RS facing, [inserting hook from back to front, work 1dc in next st to the right] to end of round, sl st in top of first st to join at the end of the round and fasten off.

FINISHING THE LID

Using 1 strand of either A or B and 3.5mm (US size E/4) hook, join yarn in any unworked front loop from Round 8 of small basket or Round 11 of large striped basket. Work a round of crab stitch around the base of the lid as for the basket and fasten off.

Take a small length of ribbon and thread from the centre back of the lid through to the centre top. Create a loop and thread the ribbon back through to the centre base of the lid. Fasten with a knot.

COTTON FACECLOTHS

These simple cotton facecloths will add a lovely homely touch to your bathroom and can be easily colour co-ordinated by matching the border shade to your décor. Worked in seed stitch they have a soft textured feel – and since they are made in 100% cotton they are fully washable.

SKILL LEVEL ●

YARN AND MATERIALS

Debbie Bliss Eco Baby (100% cotton, 125m/137yd per 50g/1¾oz ball) 5-ply (sport) weight yarn:
For one facecloth:
   2 balls of White shade 001 (A)
   1 ball of either Petal shade 053 (B) or Duck Egg shade 008 (C)

Approx. 15cm (6in) length of cotton tape per facecloth

HOOKS AND EQUIPMENT

3.5mm (US size E/4) crochet hook

Yarn needle

Sewing needle and thread

FINISHED MEASUREMENTS

Approx. 30cm (12in) x 27cm (10½in)

TENSION (GAUGE)

14 sts x 13 rows = 6.5 x 7.5cm (2½ x 3in) working pattern, using a 3.5mm (US size E/4) crochet hook.

ABBREVIATIONS

See page 127.

TIP

For a perfect handmade gift work up one or two facecloths, add a bar of sweet-smelling soap and tie up with some matching ribbon.

Facecloth

Using 3.5mm (US size E/4) hook and A, ch59.
Row 1: 1dc in second ch from hook, *1tr in next ch, 1dc in next ch; rep from * to last st, 1tr in last st, turn. *58 sts.*
Row 2: Ch1 (does not count as st), 1dc in first st, *1tr in next st, 1dc in next st; rep from * to end of row, working 1tr in last st, turn. *58 sts.*
Rep Row 2 until facecloth measures 29cm (11½in).
Fasten off.

BORDER
Round 1: With RS facing, join A in top right-hand corner of facecloth, work 1dc in each st along top edge to corner, 2dc in corner st, 1dc in each row end down left-hand side, 2dc in corner st, 1dc in each st along bottom edge, 2dc in corner st, 1dc in each row end up right-hand side, 2dc in corner st, sl st in top of first dc to join. Fasten off A.
Round 2: With RS facing, join either B or C in top right-hand corner, [1dc BLO in each st to corner, 2dc in corner st] 4 times, sl st in top of first st to join, ch1.
Round 3: Ch1 (does not count as st), *sl st in next st, ch1, sl st in next st, ch1; rep from * around entire edge of facecloth, sl st in top of first st to join.
Fasten off.

Making up and finishing

Sew in ends.
Fold length of cotton tape to make a loop and stitch this into place at one corner of the facecloth.

BOBBLY HANGER COVERS

There's something a little bit luxurious about a covered hanger but with this super-easy bobbly version, all of your hangers can be given the star treatment! The covers and bobbles can be made in any colour combination of your choice.

SKILL LEVEL ●

YARN AND MATERIALS

Debbie Bliss Baby Cashmerino (55% wool, 33% acrylic, 12% cashmere, 125m/137yd per 50g/1¾oz ball) 5-ply (sport) weight yarn:
  2 balls of Camel shade 102 (A)
  1 ball of Mustard shade 316 (B)
  Part ball each of:
  Flame shade 306 (C)
  White shade 100 (D)

NOTE

Yarn quantitites given are to make the hanger covers shown. If you want to switch colours, each cover requires one ball of the main colour and a part ball for the bobbles.

25cm (10in) of 1cm (½in) wide co-ordinating ribbon per hanger

3 wooden hangers, 44cm (17¼in) long

HOOKS AND EQUIPMENT

3.5mm (US size E/4) crochet hook

Yarn needle

FINISHED MEASUREMENTS

Width 44cm (17¼in), circumference 9cm (3½in)

TENSION (GAUGE)

15 sts x 15 rows = 6.5 x 6cm (2½ x 2⅜in) working double crochet, using a 3.5mm (US size E/4) crochet hook.

ABBREVIATIONS

See page 127.

SPECIAL ABBREVIATION

MB (make bobble): using yarn that is laid along top of row, [yarn round hook, insert hook in stitch, yarn round hook, pull yarn through work, yarn round hook, pull yarn through first 2 loops on hook] 6 times all in same stitch, using main colour yarn round hook, pull through all loops on hook

Cover

Using 3.5mm (US size E/4) hook and A or B, ch94.
Row 1 (RS): 1dc in second ch from hook, 1dc in each ch to end, turn. *93 sts.*
Rows 2–4: Ch1 (does not count as st throughout), 1dc in each st to end, turn.
Row 5: Ch1 in main colour, lay second colour of your choice along top of row, 1dc in main colour in each of next 6 sts (working over second colour), MB in second colour, *1dc in main colour in each of next 9 sts, MB in second colour; rep from * to last 6 sts, 1dc in each of last 6 sts, fasten off second colour, turn.
Rows 6–14: Ch1, 1dc in each st to end, turn. *93 sts.*
Row 15: Rep Row 5.
Row 16–19: Ch1, 1dc in each st to end, turn. *93 sts.* Fasten off.

Making up and finishing

Find the central point of the cover by folding it in half lengthways and widthways. Push the hanger hook through the centre point. Shape the cover around the hanger. Using the main colour yarn, work a dc seam down each of the short edges and along the bottom of the hanger to join the cover front to the cover back. Fasten off and sew in any ends. Add a co-ordinating colour ribbon and tie in a bow at the base of the hanger hook.

STRIPED RUFFLE BLANKET

Made in the softest of yarns this blanket is the perfect size
for a single bed but will work equally as well as a throw for
a small double bed. With its soft colourway and bands of
stripes and bobbles it will add a contemporary feel to any
bedroom. The blanket is worked in half treble crochet and
finished off with a delicate ruffle border. See page 47 for a
matching cushion.

SKILL LEVEL ● ●

YARN AND MATERIALS

Caron Simply Soft (100% acrylic, 288m/315yd per
170g/6oz ball) aran (worsted) weight yarn:
    7 balls of Victorian Rose shade 9721 (A)
    5 balls of Bone shade 9703 (B)
    2 balls of Off White shade 9702 (C)

HOOKS AND EQUIPMENT

4.5mm (US size 7) crochet hook

Yarn needle

FINISHED MEASUREMENTS

Width 128cm (50½in), length 178cm (70in)

TENSION (GAUGE)

15 sts x 15 rows = 10 x 10cm (4 x 4in) working half
treble into space between stitches, using a 4.5mm
(US size 7) crochet hook.

ABBREVIATIONS

See page 127.

SPECIAL ABBREVIATION

MB (make bobble): using yarn that is laid along top
of row, [yarn round hook, insert hook in stitch, yarn
round hook, pull yarn through work, yarn round
hook, pull yarn through first 2 loops on hook] 5 times
all in same stitch, using main colour yarn round
hook, pull through all loops on hook

NOTE

To give a denser fabric, the majority of the blanket is
worked in half treble but with each stitch being
worked into the space between stitches from the
row below, rather than into the loops of the stitch
itself. Take care to insert your hook into the correct
place as indicated by pattern and to maintain the
correct stitch count throughout.

Blanket

Using 4.5mm (US size 7) hook and A, ch191.
Row 1: 1htr in second ch from hook, 1htr in each ch to
end, turn. *190 sts.*
Rows 2–9: Ch1 (does not count as st throughout), 1htr in
each st to end working in sp between sts from row below
(see Note in Special abbreviation section, above), fasten
off A, turn.
Row 10: With RS facing join B at right-hand side of
blanket with a ch, 1htr BLO in each st to end, turn.
Rows 11–18: Ch1, 1htr in each st to end working in sp
between sts from row below, fasten off B, turn.
Row 19: With RS facing join C at right-hand side of
blanket with a ch, 1htr BLO in each st to end, turn.
Row 20: Ch1, 1htr in each st to end working in sp
between sts from row below, turn.
Row 21: Ch1, lay A along top of row, 1dc in C in each of
next 10 sts, [MB in A in next st, 1dc in C in each of next
12 sts] 13 times, MB in A in next st, 1dc in C in each of
last 10 sts, fasten off A, turn.
Rows 22–23: Ch1, 1htr in each st to end working in sp
between sts from row below, fasten off C, turn.

Row 24: With RS facing join B at right-hand side of blanket with a ch, 1htr BLO in each st to end, turn.
Rows 25–32: Rep rows 11-18.
Row 33: With RS facing join A at right-hand side of blanket with a ch, 1htr BLO in each st to end, turn.
Rows 34–41: Rep rows 2-9.
Row 42: With RS facing join C at right-hand side of blanket with a ch, 1htr BLO in each st to end, turn.
Row 43: Ch1, 1htr in each st to end working in sp between sts from row below, turn.
Row 44: Ch1, lay B along top of row, 1dc in C in each of next 10 sts, [MB in B in next st, 1dc in C in each of next 12 sts] 13 times, MB in B in next st, 1dc in C in each of last 10 sts, fasten off B, turn.
Rows 45 and 46: Ch1, 1htr in each st to end working in sp between sts from row below, fasten off C, turn.
Row 47: With RS facing join A at right-hand side of blanket with a ch, 1htr BLO in each st to end, turn.
Rows 48–55: Rep rows 2-9.
Rep Rows 10–55 four more times.
Rep Rows 10–41 once.

BORDER
Round 1: With RS facing join A at top right-hand corner of blanket, 1dc in each st along top edge, 3dc in corner st, 1dc in each row end down left-hand side, 3dc in corner st, 1dc in each st across bottom edge, 3dc in corner st, 1dc in each row end up right-hand side, 3dc in corner st, sl st in top of first dc to join.
Round 2: Ch1, [1dc in each st to corner, 3dc in corner st] 4 times, sl st in ch-1 to join.
Round 3: Ch1, 2dc in each st around blanket, sl st in top of ch-1 to join.
Round 4: Rep Round 3.
Fasten off.

Making up and finishing

Sew in all ends.

STRIPED RUFFLE CUSHION

Made to match the single bed blanket on page 44, this little rectangular cushion will add the finishing touch to your bed. The cover has a simple overlap fold at the back so the cushion pad can be removed easily. The cushion is worked in half treble crochet and finished off with a delicate ruffle border down each side.

SKILL LEVEL ● ●

YARN AND MATERIALS

Caron Simply Soft (100% acrylic, 288m/315yd per 170g/6oz ball) aran (worsted) weight yarn:
  1 ball in each of:
  Victorian Rose shade 9721 (A)
  Bone shade 9703 (B)
  Off White shade 9702 (C)

30 x 40cm (12 x 16in) cushion pad

HOOKS AND EQUIPMENT

4.5mm (US size 7) crochet hook

Yarn needle

FINISHED MEASUREMENTS

Width 46cm (18in), height 31cm (12¼in)

TENSION (GAUGE)

15 sts x 15 rows = 10 x 10cm (4 x 4in) working half treble into space between stitches, using a 4.5mm (US size 7) crochet hook.

ABBREVIATIONS

See page 127.

SPECIAL ABBREVIATION

MB (make bobble): using yarn that is laid along top of row, [yarn round hook, insert hook in stitch, yarn round hook, pull yarn through work, yarn round hook, pull yarn through first 2 loops on hook] 5 times all in same stitch, using main colour yarn round hook, pull through all loops on hook

NOTE

To give a denser fabric, the majority of the cushion is worked in half treble but with each stitch being worked into the space between stitches from the row below, rather than into the loops of the stitch itself. Take care to insert your hook into the correct place as indicated by pattern and to maintain the correct stitch count throughout.

Cushion

Using 4.5mm (US size 7) hook and B, ch110.
Row 1: 1htr in second ch from hook, 1htr in each ch to end, turn. *109 sts.*
Rows 2–5: Ch1 (does not count as st throughout), 1htr in each st to end working in sp between sts from row below (see Note in Special abbreviation section), fasten off B, turn.
Row 6: With RS facing join C at right-hand side of blanket with a ch, 1htr BLO in each st to end, turn.
Row 7: Ch1, 1htr in each st to end working in sp between sts from row below, turn.
Row 8: Ch1, lay A along top of row, 1dc in C in each of next 15 sts, [MB in A in next st, 1dc in C in each of next 12 sts] 6 times, MB in A in next st, 1dc in C in each of next 15 sts, fasten off A, turn.
Rows 9–10: Ch1, 1htr in each st to end working in sp between sts from row below, fasten off C, turn.
Row 11: With RS facing join B at right-hand side of blanket with a ch, 1htr BLO in each st to end, turn.
Rows 12–19: Ch1, 1htr in each to end working in sp between sts from row below, fasten off B, turn.
Row 20: With RS facing join A at right-hand side of blanket with a ch, 1htr BLO in each st to end, turn.

Rows 21–28: Ch1, 1htr in each st to end working in sp between sts from row below, fasten off A, turn.

Row 29: With RS facing join C at right-hand side of blanket with a ch, 1htr BLO in each st to end, turn.

Row 30: Ch1, 1htr in each st to end working in sp between sts from row below, turn.

Row 31: Ch1, lay B along top of row, 1dc in C in each of next 10 sts [MB in B in next st, 1dc in C in each of next 12 sts] 13 times, MB in B in next st, 1dc in C in each of last 10 sts, fasten off B, turn.

Rows 32 and 33: Ch1, 1htr in each st to end working in sp between sts from row below, fasten off C, turn.

Rows 34–42: Rep Rows 20–28.

Rows 43–51: Rep Rows 11–19.

Rows 52–57: Rep Rows 6–11.

Rows 58–61: Ch1, 1 htr in each st to end working in sp between sts from row below.

Fasten off B.

BORDER

Round 1: With RS facing, rejoin B at top right-hand corner of cushion cover, 1dc in each st along top edge, 2dc in corner st, 1dc in each row end down left-hand side, 2dc in corner st, 1dc in each st across bottom edge, 2dc in corner st, 1dc in each row end up right-hand side, 2dc in corner st, sl st in top of first dc to join. Fasten off.

> TIP
>
> You will find that once the cushion pad is inside the cover the overlap is deep enough not to need any fastenings to hold it in place.

Making up and finishing

Lay the cushion cover on a flat surface, RS down. Place the cushion pad in the middle, fold the bottom of the cover up and the top of the cover down so that the cushion pad is enclosed, and the two edges overlap. Pin across the join at the back of the cushion where the opening will be – this will hold the cover in place whilst you pin the sides together. Once one side is pinned take the cushion pad out and pin the second side.

JOIN SIDE AND ADD RUFFLE EDGE

With RS facing, using 4.5mm (US size 7) hook and A, work a dc seam down one side joining the front and back edges together, making sure you work through all 3 layers where the opening overlaps. Do not fasten off, turn.

Ruffle edge row 1: Ch1 (does not count as st throughout), 2dc in each st to end of side, turn.

Ruffle edge row 2: Ch1, 2dc in each st to end of side. Fasten off.

Rep to join and add ruffle edge to second side.

HOT WATER BOTTLE COVER

Nothing quite beats snuggling up with a hot water bottle on a cold night – and when it's tucked inside this cosy cover both you and the hot water bottle will stay toasty and warm for hours. Worked as a simple rectangle, the cover is a generous fit for all standard-sized hot water bottles.

SKILL LEVEL ● ●

YARN AND MATERIALS
Debbie Bliss Baby Cashmerino (55% wool, 33% acrylic, 12% cashmere, 125m/137yd per 50g/1¾oz ball) 5-ply (sport) weight yarn:
  2 balls each of:
  Flame shade 306 (A)
  Mustard shade 316 (D)
  1 ball each of:
  Camel shade 102 (B)
  White shade 100 (C)

50cm (19¾in) of 22mm (⅞in) wide co-ordinating ribbon

1 hot water bottle, standard size

HOOKS AND EQUIPMENT
3.5mm (US size E/4) crochet hook

Yarn needle

FINISHED MEASUREMENTS
Width 21cm (8¼in), length 38cm (15in)

TENSION (GAUGE)
15 sts x 15 rows = 6.5 x 6cm (2½ x 2⅜in) working double crochet, using a 3.5mm (US size E/4) crochet hook.

ABBREVIATIONS
See page 127.

SPECIAL ABBREVIATION
MB (make bobble): using yarn that is laid along top of row, [yarn round hook, insert hook in stitch, yarn round hook, pull yarn through work, yarn round hook, pull yarn through first 2 loops on hook] 4 times all in same stitch, using main colour yarn round hook, pull through all loops on hook

Cover
Using 3.5mm (US size E/4) hook and A, ch91.
Row 1: 1dc in second ch from hook, 1dc in each ch to end. *90 sts.*
Turn at end of this row and every foll row. Do not fasten off a yarn until instructed to do so, instead carry it loosely up the side between rows. Unless otherwise indicated, the colour used for the first ch1 of each row should be used for the remainder of the row; join new colours when necessary.
Rows 2–4: Ch1 (does not count as a st throughout), 1dc in each st to end.
Rows 5–6: Ch1 in D, 1dc in each st to end.
Row 7: Ch1 in A, 1dc in each st to end, fasten off A.
Row 8: Ch1 in B, 1dc in each st to end.
Row 9: Ch1 in B, lay D along top of row, 1dc in B in each of next 4 sts, MB in D, *1dc in B in each of next 8 sts, MB in D; rep from * to last 4 sts, 1dc in B in each of last 4 sts.
Row 10: Ch1 in B, 1dc in each st to end, fasten off B.
Row 11: Ch1 in A, 1dc in each st to end, fasten off A.
Rows 12–13: Ch1 in D, 1dc in each st to end.
Row 14: Ch1 in C, lay B along top of row, *1dc in C in each of next 2 sts working yrh of last st in B, 1dc in B in each of next 2 sts working yrh of last st in C; rep from * to last 2 sts, 1dc in C in each of last 2 sts working yrh of last st in B.
Row 15: Ch1 in B, lay C along top of row, *1dc in B in each of next 2 sts working yrh of last st in C, 1dc in C in each of next 2 sts working yrh of last st in B; rep from * to last 2 sts, 1dc in B in each of last 2 sts, fasten off B and C.
Rows 16–18: Ch1 in A, 1dc in each st to end.
Row 19: Ch1 in D, 1dc in each st to end, fasten off D.
Row 20: Ch1 in B, 1dc in each st to end.
Row 21: Ch1 in B, lay A along top of row, 1dc in B in each of next 4 sts, MB in A, *1dc in B in each of next 8 sts, MB in A; rep from * to last 4 sts, 1dc in B in each of last 4 sts.
Row 22: Ch1 in B, 1dc in each st to end, fasten off B.
Row 23: Ch1 in D, 1dc in each st to end, fasten off D.
Rows 24–25: Ch1 in A, 1dc in each st to end, fasten off A.
Rows 26–27: Rep Rows 14 and 15.
Rows 28–30: Ch1 in D, 1dc in each st to end.
Row 31: Ch1 in A, 1dc in each st to end, fasten off A.
Row 32: Ch1 in B, 1dc in each st to end.

Row 33: Ch1 in B, lay D along top of row, 1dc in B in each of next 4 sts, MB in D, *1dc in B in each of next 8 sts, MB in D; rep from * to last 4 sts, 1dc in B in each of last 4 sts.
Row 34: Ch1 in B, 1dc in each st to end, fasten off B.
Row 35: Ch1 in A, 1dc in each st to end, fasten off A.
Rows 36–37: Ch1 in D, 1dc in each st to end, fasten off D.
Rows 38–61: Rep Rows 14–37.
Rows 62–83: Rep Rows 14–35.
Rows 84–85: Ch1 in D, 1dc in each st to end.
Row 86 (eyelet row): Ch1 in D, 1dc in each of next 5 sts, *ch3, miss next 3 sts, 1dc in each of next 4 sts; rep from * to last 8 sts, ch3, miss next 3 sts, 1dc in each of last 5 sts.
Rows 87–88: Ch1 in D, 1dc in each st to end.
Row 89: Join in C, ch1, lay B along top of row, *1dc in C in each of next 2 sts working yrh of last st in B, 1dc in B in each of next 2 sts working yrh of last st in C; rep from * to last 2 sts, 1dc in C in each of last 2 sts working yrh of last st in B.
Row 90: Ch1 in B, lay C along top of row, *1dc in B in each of next 2 sts working yrh of last st in C, 1dc in C in each of next 2 sts working yrh of last st in B; rep from * to last 2 sts, 1dc in B in each of last 2 sts, fasten off B and C.
Rows 91–94: Ch1 in A, 1dc in each st to end.
Row 95: Ch1 in D, 1dc in each st to end, fasten off D.
Row 96: Ch1 in B, 1dc in each st to end.
Row 97: Ch1 in B, lay A along top of row, 1dc in B in each of next 4 sts, MB in A, *1dc in B in each of next 8 sts, MB in A; rep from * to last 4 sts, 1dc in B in each of last 4 sts.
Row 98: Ch1 in B, 1dc in each st to end.

Row 99: Ch1 in D, 1dc in each st to end.
Rows 100–101: Ch1 in A, 1dc in each st to end, fasten off A.
Rows 102–103: Rep Rows 14–15.
Row 104: Ch1 in D, 1dc in each st to end.
Fasten off.

Making up and finishing

EDGING
With the RS of the work facing, using a 3.5mm (US size E/4) hook, join D in the top left-hand corner of the cover.
Row 1 (RS): Work 1dc in each row end down left-hand edge, turn.
Row 1 (WS): Ch1, 1dc in each st to end.
Fasten off.
Rep for the right-hand edge of the cover.

Sew in or knot together all ends on the inside of the cover.

With WS together and using D, join the two side edges together with a dc seam – this seam will be a feature on the centre back of the cover. Centre the dc seam on one side, turn the cover WS out and sew the bottom edge closed. Turn RS out again.

Place the hot water bottle inside. Thread co-ordinating ribbon through the eyelets (Row 86), with the two ends meeting centre front, and tie the ends in a bow.

CHAPTER 3

LIVING ROOM

BOBBLY SOFA THROW

When the evenings get chilly, or you just fancy an afternoon curled up on the sofa, this throw is all you need to get cosy. Made in chunky yarn, it is beautifully warm and the bobbles and pompoms add a contemporary twist to a simple blanket.

SKILL LEVEL ● ●

YARN AND MATERIALS

Paintbox Yarns Wool Mix Chunky (50% wool, 50% acrylic, 100m/109yd per 100g/3½oz ball) chunky (bulky) weight yarn:
   23 balls of Pistachio Green shade 1024 (A)

Paintbox Yarns Wool Mix Aran (50% wool, 50% acrylic, 180m/197yd per 100g/3½oz ball) aran (worsted) weight yarn:
   2 balls of Paper White shade 800 (B)

HOOKS AND EQUIPMENT

6mm (US size J/10) crochet hook

Yarn needle

45mm (1¾in) pompom maker

FINISHED MEASUREMENTS

Width 112cm (44in), length 142cm (56in)

TENSION (GAUGE)

15 sts x 15 rows = 12cm x 9cm (4¾in x 3½in) working double crochet, using a 6mm (US size J/10) crochet hook with A.

ABBREVIATIONS

See page 127.

SPECIAL ABBREVIATION

MB (make bobble): using B, [yarn round hook, insert hook in stitch, yarn round hook, pull yarn through work, yarn round hook, pull yarn through first 2 loops on hook] 5 times all in same stitch, yarn round hook in A and pull through all loops on hook.

> ### TIP
>
> It will be easier to weave in the ends after attaching the pompoms if you use yarn A for the central tie, as then the ends will blend in with the main colour of the throw better.

Throw

Using A, ch144.
Row 1: 1dc in second ch from hook, 1dc in each ch to end, turn. *143 sts.*
Rows 2–6: Ch1 (does not count as st throughout), 1dc in each of next 143 sts, turn.
*Row 7 (bobble row 1): Ch1, lay B along top of row as you work, using A, 1dc in each of next 7 sts (working over B), using B, MB in next st, [using A, 1dc in each of next 15 sts, using B, MB in the next st] 8 times, using A, 1dc in each of last 7 sts.
Fasten off B at end of row.
Rows 8–22: Rep Row 2.
Row 23 (bobble row 2): Ch1, lay B along top of row as you work, [using A, 1dc in each of next 15 sts, using B, MB in next st] 8 times, using A, 1dc in each of last 15 sts.
Fasten off B at end of row.
Rows 24–38: Rep Row 2.**
Repeat from * to ** until you have worked a total of 14 bobble rows, ending with Bobble Row 2.
Work a further 6 rows of dc, ending on a RS row.
Do not fasten off, do not turn.

BORDER

Round 1: Work a second dc in last st of row (corner made), work 1dc in each row end down left-hand side, 2dc in corner st, work 1dc in each st along bottom edge, 2dc in corner st, work 1dc in each row end up right-hand side of blanket, 2dc in corner st, sl st in top of first st of last row of blanket to join.
Round 2: Ch1, with RS still facing work crab stitch clockwise around edge of throw as follows: [inserting hook from back to front, work 1dc in next st to the right] to end of round, sl st in ch-1 to join at end of round.
Fasten off.

Making up and finishing

Sew in all ends.
Using B and a 45mm (1¾in) pompom maker make 18 pompoms, leaving a long tail on the central tie of each pompom. Attach 9 pompoms evenly along the top and bottom edge of the throw.

COFFEE TABLE COASTER SET

Add a little colour to your coffee table with these cheery coasters. When not in use they can be stacked up in the matching basket to keep them tidied away.

SKILL LEVEL ●

YARN AND MATERIALS

Wool and the Gang Shiny Happy Cotton (100% cotton, 142m/155yd per 100g/3½oz ball) aran (worsted) weight yarn:
1 ball of Eucalyptus Green (A)
1 ball of Red Ochre (B)

Rowan Cotton Glacé (100% cotton, 115m/126yd per 50g/1¾oz ball) DK (light worsted) weight yarn:
1 ball of Blood Orange shade 445 (C)

HOOKS AND EQUIPMENT

5mm (US size H/8) crochet hook

3mm (US size C/2–D/3) crochet hook

Yarn needle

FINISHED MEASUREMENTS

Coasters: diameter 12cm (4¾in)

Basket: diameter 13cm (5¼in), height 3.5cm (1½in)

TENSION (GAUGE)

Rounds 1–4 of Coaster = 5cm (2in) diameter, using a 5mm (US size H/8) crochet hook and A.

ABBREVIATIONS

See page 127.

Coaster

(make 6)
Using 5mm (US size H/8) hook and A, make a magic ring.
Round 1: 6dc in ring, sl st in top of first dc to join. *6 sts.*
Round 2: Ch1 (does not count as st throughout), [2dc in next st] 6 times, sl st in top of ch-1 to join. *12 sts.*
Round 3: Ch1, [1dc in next st, 2dc in next st] 6 times, sl st in top of ch-1 to join. *18 sts.*
Round 4: Ch1, 1dc in first st, 2dc in next st, [1dc in each of next 2 sts, 2dc in next st] 5 times, 1dc in last st, sl st in top of ch-1 to join. *24 sts.*
Round 5: Ch1, [1dc in each of next 3 sts, 2dc in next st] 6 times, sl st in top of ch-1 to join. *30 sts.*
Round 6: Ch1, 1dc in each of next 2 sts, 2dc in next st, [1dc in each of next 4 sts, 2dc in next st] 5 times, 1dc in each of next 2 sts, sl st in top of ch-1 to join. *36 sts.*
Round 7: Ch1, [1dc in each of next 5 sts, 2dc in next st] 6 times, sl st in top of ch-1 to join. *42 sts.*
Round 8: Ch1, 1dc in each of next 3 sts, 2dc in next st, [1dc in each of next 6 sts, 2dc in next st] 5 times, 1dc in each of next 3 sts, sl st in top of ch-1 to join. *48 sts.*
Fasten off A.

BORDER

Using 3mm (US size C/2–D/3) hook, with RS facing, join in C with a sl st to any st around edge of coaster.
Round 1: Ch1, *1dc in next st, 2dc in next st; rep from * around edge of coaster, sl st in ch-1 to join. *72 sts.*
Round 2: Ch1, working in back loops only, sl st in next st, *ch1, sl st in next st; rep from * around edge of coaster, sl st in ch-1 to join.
Fasten off C.

TIP

When working the rounds, finish each round by joining back to the beginning with a slip stitch. Chain 1 and work the first stitch from the next round in the double crochet at the base of the chain. This will give you a straight, neat join at the end of each round.

Basket

Using 5mm (US size H/8) hook and B, make a magic ring.
Rounds 1–8: Work as Rounds 1–8 of coaster. *48 sts.*
Round 9: Ch1, [1dc in each of next 7 sts, 2dc in next st] 6 times, sl st in top of ch-1 to join. *54 sts.*
Round 10: Ch1, 1dc in each of next 4 sts, 2dc in next st, [1dc in each of next 8 sts, 2dc in next st] 5 times, 1dc in each of next 4 sts, sl st in top of ch-1 to join. *60 sts.*
Round 11: Ch1, [1dc in each of next 9 sts, 2dc in next st] 6 times, sl st in top of ch-1 to join. *66 sts.*
Round 12: Ch1, 1dc in each of next 5 sts, 2dc in next st, [1dc in each of next 10 sts, 2dc in next st] 5 times, 1dc in each of next 5 sts, sl st in top of ch-1 to join. *72 sts.*
Round 13: Ch1, turn work so that underside of basket base is facing you, working in back loops only, 1dc in each st around, sl st in top of first st of round, do not turn.
Round 14: Ch1, now working in both loops again as usual, 1dc in each st around, sl st in top of ch-1 to join.
Rounds 15–19: Rep Round 14.
Fasten off.

Making up and finishing

FINISHING THE COASTER

Using 3mm (US size C/2–D/3) hook and C, with RS facing, work a round of sl st one round in from the border, inserting hook right through the coaster.
Fasten off.

FINISHING THE BASKET

Using 3mm (US size C/2–D/3) hook, with RS facing, join C with a sl st in any st around top edge of basket, ch1, sl st in next st, *ch1, sl st in the next st, rep from * around edge of basket, sl st in top of ch-1 to join.
Fasten off.
Using 3mm (US size C/2–D/3) hook and A, with RS facing, work a round of sl st one round down from the border, inserting hook right through the side of the basket.
Fasten off.

TEXTURED CUSHION WITH POMPOMS

This rectangular cushion is worked in alpine stitch, to match the textured lap blanket on page 62. The cushion is finished with a pompom at each corner as a fun touch and to keep it co-ordinating with the blanket.

SKILL LEVEL ●

YARN AND MATERIALS

Lion Brand Wool Ease (80% acrylic, 20% wool, 180m/197yd per 85g/3oz ball) aran (worsted) weight yarn:
   3 balls of Natural Heather
      shade 098 (A)
   1 ball of Fisherman shade 099 (B)

40 x 30cm (16 x 12in) cushion pad

3 snap fasteners

3 buttons

HOOKS AND EQUIPMENT

5.5mm (US size I/9) crochet hook

Yarn needle

35mm (1½in) pompom maker

FINISHED MEASUREMENTS

Width 40cm (16in), height 30cm (12in)

TENSION (GAUGE)

15 sts x 15 rows = 10.5 x 10cm (4¼ x 4in) working Rows 1–3 and then Rows 4–7 three times, using a 5.5mm (US size I/9) crochet hook.

ABBREVIATIONS

See page 127.

SPECIAL ABBREVIATION

FPtr (front post treble): yarn round hook, from front of work insert hook from right to left behind post of next st on prev round and through to front again, yarn round hook and pull loop through, [yarn round hook, draw through 2 loops] twice

Cushion cover

Using 5.5mm (US size I/9) hook and A, ch60.
Row 1 (WS): 1dc in second ch from hook, 1dc in each ch to end, turn. *59 sts.*
Row 2 (RS): Ch2 (does not count as st throughout), 1tr in each st to end, turn.
Row 3: Ch1 (does not count as st throughout), 1dc in each st to end, turn.
Row 4: Ch2, *1FPtr in next st, 1tr in next st; rep from * to last st, 1tr in last st, turn.
Row 5: Ch1, 1dc in each st to end, turn.
Row 6: Ch2, 1tr in first st, *1FPtr in next st, 1tr in next st; rep from * to end, turn.
Row 7: Ch1, 1dc in each st to end, turn.
Rep Rows 4–7 until work measures 66cm (26in), ending on a dc row, turn.
Final row: Ch1, 1dc in each st to end, do not turn.

BORDER

Round 1: Work a second dc in last st of prev row (corner made), work 1dc in each row end down left-hand side, 2dc in corner st, work 1dc in each st along bottom edge, 2dc in corner st, work 1dc in each row end up right-hand side of cushion, 2dc in corner st, sl st in top of first st of last row of cushion to join.
Fasten off.
Round 2: Join B in top right corner, *2dc in corner st, 1dc in each st to corner; rep from * 3 times, sl st in top of first dc to join.
Fasten off.

Making up and finishing

Lay the cushion cover on a flat surface, RS down. Place the cushion pad in the middle, fold the bottom of the cover up and the top of the cover down so that the cushion pad is enclosed, and the two edges overlap. Pin across the join at the back of the cushion where the opening will be. Pin the sides.

JOIN SIDES

Row 1 (RS): Using 5.5mm (US size I/9) hook, with RS of cushion facing and using B, work a dc seam to join layers down one side, do not fasten off, do not turn.
Row 2: Ch1, work crab stitch clockwise with RS facing as foll: [inserting hook from back to front, work 1dc in next st to the right] up side of cushion.
Fasten off.
Rep on other side of cushion.

Sew in any ends.

Using pompom maker and B, make 4 pompoms.
Stitch one pompom securely to each corner.

Stitch the three snap fasteners into place so that the opening of the cushion is closed, and the fasteners are hidden underneath the overlapping flap. Using a sewing needle and thread, sew the three buttons onto the back of the cushion, directly above where the fasteners are.

TEXTURED LAP BLANKET

This beautifully soft blanket is worked in alpine stitch, which creates a wonderful texture whilst still giving lots of drape. It's perfect for laying over your knees on a chilly evening to add a little warmth – but without the bulk and heaviness of a larger blanket. See page 59 for the matching cushion.

SKILL LEVEL ●

YARN AND MATERIALS

Lion Brand Wool Ease (80% acrylic, 20% wool, 180m/197yd per 85g/3oz ball) aran (worsted) weight yarn:
    10 balls of Natural Heather shade 098 (A)
    1 ball of Fisherman shade 099 (B)

HOOKS AND EQUIPMENT

5.5mm (US size I/9) crochet hook

Yarn needle

68mm (2½in) pompom maker

FINISHED MEASUREMENTS

102cm (40in) square

TENSION (GAUGE)

15 sts x 15 rows = 10.5 x 10cm (4¼ x 4in) working Rows 1–3 and then Rows 4–7 three times, using a 5.5mm (US size I/9) crochet hook.

ABBREVIATIONS

See page 127.

SPECIAL ABBREVIATION

FPtr (front post treble): yarn round hook, from front of work insert hook from right to left behind post of next st on prev round and through to front again, yarn round hook and pull loop through, [yarn round hook, draw through 2 loops] twice

Blanket

Using 5.5mm (US size I/9) hook and A, ch152.
Row 1 (WS): 1dc in second ch from hook, 1dc in each ch to end, turn. *151 sts.*
Row 2 (RS): Ch2 (does not count as st throughout), 1tr in each st to end, turn.
Row 3: Ch1 (does not count as st throughout), 1dc in each st to end, turn.
Row 4: Ch2, *1FPtr in next st, 1tr in next st; rep from * to last st, 1tr in last st, turn.
Row 5: Ch1, 1dc in each st to end, turn.
Row 6: Ch2, 1tr in first st, *1FPtr in next st, 1tr in next st; rep from * to end, turn.
Row 7: Ch1, 1dc in each st to end, turn.
Rep Rows 4–7 until work measures 95cm (37½in), ending on a dc row.
Final row: Ch1, 1dc in each st to end. Fasten off.

SIDE BORDER

Using 5.5mm (US size I/9) hook and with RS facing, join yarn A at top corner of one side edge.
Row 1: 1dc in each row end down side edge, turn.
Row 2: Ch1, 1dc in each st to end. Fasten off.
Rep for second side.

EDGING

Using 5.5mm (US size I/9) hook and with RS facing, join B at top right-hand corner.
Round 1: *2dc in first st (corner made), 1dc in each st to corner; rep from * 3 times, sl st in top of first dc to join.
Round 2: Ch1, work crab stitch clockwise with RS facing as foll: [inserting hook from back to front, work 1dc in next st to the right] to end of round, sl st in top of first st to join. Fasten off.

Making up and finishing

Sew in ends.
Using pompom maker and B, make 4 pompoms.
Stitch one pompom securely to each corner.

STRIPED BOLSTER CUSHION

How about creating some variation in your cushion collection by adding in a bolster? Incredibly comfortable and just a little bit different, this bobbly, textured cover will fit perfectly in any room and can be made in a multitude of colourways.

SKILL LEVEL ● ●

YARN AND MATERIALS

Debbie Bliss Baby Cashmerino (55% wool, 33% acrylic, 12% cashmere, 125m/137yd per 50g/1¾oz ball) 5-ply (sport) weight yarn:

2 balls each of:
Mist shade 057 (A)
Denim shade 027 (D)
Lagoon shade 310 (F)
1 ball each of:
Camel shade 102 (B)
White shade 100 (C)
Mink shade 064 (E)

3 snap fasteners

45cm (18in) x 20cm (8in) bolster cushion pad

HOOKS AND EQUIPMENT

3.5mm (US size E/4) crochet hook

Stitch marker

Yarn needle

FINISHED MEASUREMENTS

Length 47cm (18½in), diameter 24cm (9½in)

TENSION (GAUGE)

15 sts x 15 rows = 6.5 x 6cm (2½ x 2⅜in) working double crochet, using a 3.5mm (US size E/4) crochet hook.

ABBREVIATIONS

See page 127.

SPECIAL ABBREVIATION

MB (make bobble): using yarn that is laid along top of row, [yarn round hook, insert hook in stitch, yarn round hook, pull yarn through work, yarn round hook, pull yarn through first 2 loops on hook] 5 times all in same stitch, using main colour yarn round hook, pull through all loops on hook

Cover

Using 3.5mm (US size E/4) hook and A, ch97.

Turn at end of this row and every foll row. Do not fasten off a yarn until instructed to do so, instead carry it loosely up the side between rows. Unless otherwise indicated, the colour used for the first ch1 of each row should be used for the remainder of the row; join new colours when necessary.

Row 1: 1dc in second ch from hook, 1dc in each ch to end, turn. *96 sts.*

Rows 2–12: Ch1 (does not count as st throughout), 1dc in each st to end, turn.

Row 13: Ch2 (does not count as st throughout) in B, 1tr in each st to end, fasten off B, turn.

Row 14: Ch1 in C, 1dc in each st to end, turn.

Row 15: Ch1, lay A along top of row, 1dc in C in each of next 2 sts, MB in A, *1dc in C in each of next 6 sts, MB in A; rep from * to last 2 sts, 1dc in C in each of last 2 sts, fasten off A, turn.

Rows 16–17: Ch1 in C, 1dc in each st to end, fasten off C, turn.

Row 18: Ch1 in B, 1dc in each st to end, turn.
Row 19: Ch2, 1tr in each st to end, fasten off B, turn.
Row 20: Ch2 in D, 1htr in first st, miss next st, 2htr in next st, *miss next st, 2htr in next st; rep from * to last st, 1htr in last st, fasten off D, turn.
Row 21: Ch2 in C, 1htr in first st, *miss next st, 2htr in sp between 2 htr from prev row; rep from * to last st, 1htr in last st, fasten off C, turn.
Row 22: Ch2 in D, rep Row 21, fasten off D, turn.
Row 23: Ch2 in E, 1tr in each st to end, turn.
Row 24: Ch1, 1dc in each st to end, fasten off E, turn.
Rows 25–26: Ch1 in F, 1dc in each st to end, turn.
Row 27: Ch1, lay C along top of row, 1dc in F in each of next 2 sts, MB in C, *1dc in F in each of next 6 sts, MB in C; rep from * to last 2 sts, 1dc in F in each of last 2 sts, fasten off C, turn.
Row 28: Ch1 in F, 1dc in each st to end, fasten off F, turn.
Row 29: Ch2 in E, 1tr in each st to end, fasten off E, turn.
Rows 30–32: Ch1 in A, 1dc in each st to end, fasten off A, turn.
Row 33: Ch2 in F, 1htr in each st to end, turn.
Row 34: Ch1, 1dc in each st to end, turn.
Rows 35–36: Ch1 in C, 1dc in each st to end, fasten off C, turn.

Row 37: Ch2 in F, 1htr in each st to end, fasten off F, turn.
Row 38: Ch1 in D, 1dc in each st to end, fasten off D, turn.
Rep Rows 13–38 four more times.
Fasten off.

EDGING
Using 3.5mm (US size E/4) hook and E, work 1 row of dc evenly down each long edge.
Fasten off.

Circular ends

(make 2)
Using 3.5mm (US size E/4) hook and D, make a magic ring.
Round 1: 6dc into ring. 6 sts.
Work in a continuous spiral. PM in last st and move up as each round is finished.
Round 2: [2dc in next st] 6 times. *12 sts.*
Round 3: [1dc in next st, 2dc in next st] 6 times. *18 sts.*
Round 4: 1dc in first st, 2dc in next st, [1dc in each of next 2 sts, 2dc in next st] 5 times, 1dc in last st. *24 sts.*
Round 5: [1dc in each of next 3 sts, 2dc in next st] 6 times. *30 sts.*
Round 6: 1dc in each of first 2 sts, 2dc in next st, [1dc in each of next 4 sts, 2dc in next st] 5 times, 1dc in each of last 2 sts. *36 sts.*

Round 7: [1 dc in each of next 5 sts, 2dc in next st] 6 times. *42 sts.*

Round 8: 1dc in each of first 3 sts, 2dc in next st, [1dc in each of next 6 sts, 2dc in next st] 5 times, 1dc in each of last 3 sts. *48 sts.*

Round 9: [1dc in each of next 7 sts, 2dc in next st] 6 times. *54 sts.*

Round 10: 1dc in each of first 4 sts, 2dc in next st, [1dc in each of next 8 sts, 2dc in next st] 5 times, 1dc in each of last 4 sts. *60 sts.*

Round 11: [1dc in each of next 9 sts, 2dc in next st] 6 times. *66 sts.*

Round 12: 1dc in each of first 5 sts, 2dc in next st, [1dc in each of next 10 sts, 2dc in next st] 5 times, 1dc in each of last 5 sts. *72 sts.*

Round 13: [1dc in each of next 11 sts, 2dc in next st] 6 times. *78 sts.*

Round 14: 1dc in each of first 6 sts, 2dc in next st, [1dc in each of next 12 sts, 2dc in next st) 5 times, 1dc in each of last 6 sts. *84 sts.*

Round 15: [1dc in each of next 13 sts, 2dc in next st] 6 times. *90 sts.*

Round 16: 1dc in each of first 7 sts, 2dc in next st, [1dc in each of next 14 sts, 2dc in next st] 5 times, 1dc in each of last 7 sts. *96 sts.*

Round 17: [1dc in each of next 15 sts, 2dc in next st] 6 times. *102 sts.*

Round 18: 1dc in each of first 8 sts, 2dc in next st, [1dc in each of next 16 sts, 2dc in next st] 5 times, 1dc in each of last 8 sts. *108 sts.*

Round 19: [1dc in each of next 17 sts, 2dc in next st] 6 times. *114 sts.*

Round 20: 1dc in each of first 9 sts, 2dc in next st, [1dc in each of next 18 sts, 2dc in next st] 5 times, 1dc in each of last 9 sts. *120 sts.*

Round 21: [1dc in each of next 19 sts, 2dc in next st] 6 times. *126 sts.*

Round 22: 1dc in each of first 10 sts, 2dc in next st, [1dc in each of next 20 sts, 2dc in next st] 5 times, 1dc in each of last 10 sts. *132 sts.*

Round 23: [1dc in each of next 21 sts, 2dc in next st] 6 times. *138 sts.*

Round 24: 1dc in each of first 11 sts, 2dc in next st, [1dc in each of next 22 sts, 2dc in next st] 5 times, 1dc in each of last 11 sts. *144 sts.*

Round 25: [1dc in each of next 23 sts, 2dc in next st] 6 times. *150 sts.*

Round 26: 1dc in each of first 12 sts, 2dc in next st, [1dc in each of next 24 sts, 2dc in next st] 5 times, 1dc in each of last 12 sts, sl st in top of first dc to join round. *156 sts.* Fasten off.

Making up and finishing

With WS together, pin the circular ends along the two long edges of the cover so that you make a tube shape. As you come to the end of the circular base there will be extra length on the straight edges – this will form the overlap insert for the cushion pad.

Using 3.5mm (US size E/4) hook and D, work a dc seam all the way around the edge of the two ends, joining all the pieces together and ensuring you have worked through all the layers where the overlap meets.

RUFFLE EDGE
Using 3.5mm (US size E/4) hook, join A in any st along one circular edge.
Round 1: Ch2, 4tr in each st to end, sl st in top of beg ch-2 to join.
Fasten off.
Rep on other circular end.

Place the bolster cushion pad inside the cover and stitch the three snap fasteners evenly spaced along the inside of the overlap to close the cover.

SQUARE STORAGE BASKET

This fun storage solution is made from recycled T-shirt yarn. Working with two strands of the yarn and an 8mm crochet hook you can make it in no time at all and it is perfect for storing magazines, blankets, towels or any other loose odds and ends looking for a home.

SKILL LEVEL ●

YARN AND MATERIALS

Paintbox Yarns Recycled T-Shirt (90% cotton, 10% synthetic, 110m/120yd per 800g/28¼oz ball) super chunky (super bulky) weight yarn:
   3 balls of Off White shade 003 (A)

Paintbox Yarns Recycled Ribbon (60% cotton, 40% polyester, 120m/131yd per 250g/8¾oz ball) super chunky (super bulky) weight yarn:
   1 ball of Mustard shade 017 (B)

HOOKS AND EQUIPMENT

8mm (US size L/11) crochet hook

6mm (US size J/10) crochet hook

Large pins/safety pins

Large yarn needle

Locking stitch marker

Sewing needle and thread

FINISHED MEASUREMENTS

Width 35cm (13¾in), length 35cm (13¾in), depth 26cm (10¼in)

TENSION (GAUGE)

5 sts x 5 rows = 9.5 x 9.5cm (3¾ x 3¾in) working double crochet, using an 8mm (US size L/11) crochet hook and 2 strands of Paintbox Yarns Recycled T-Shirt held together.

ABBREVIATIONS

See page 127.

Basket

BASE
Using 8mm (US size L/11) hook and 2 strands of A held tog, ch17.
Row 1: 1dc in second ch from hook, 1dc in each ch to end, turn. *16 sts.*
Row 2: Ch1 (does not count as st throughout), 1dc in each st to end, turn.
Rows 3–15: Rep Row 2.
Row 16: Ch1, 1dc in each st to last st, (1dc, 1ch, 1dc) in last st, cont down left-hand side 15dc evenly to corner, (1dc, 1ch, 1dc) in corner, 1dc in each st along bottom edge to last st, (1dc, 1ch, 1dc) in last st, work 15dc evenly up right-hand side to corner, (1dc, 1ch, 1dc) in corner, sl st in top of ch-1 to join. *68 sts.*
Fasten off.

SIDES
With RS facing, using 8mm (US size L/11) hook and 2 strands of A held tog, join yarn in any dc immediately to the left of a ch-1 sp.
Row 1: Ch1, 1dc BLO in each of next 17 sts, turn. *17 sts.*
Row 2: Ch1, working in both loops, 1dc in each of 17 sts, turn.
Rows 3–15: Rep Row 2.
Fasten off.
Rep on other sides of base to work other 3 sides.

Handles

(make 2)
Using 8mm (US size L/11) hook and 2 strands of A held tog, ch36.
Row 1: 1dc in second ch from hook, 1dc in each ch to end. *35 sts.*
Fasten off.

Star

(make 4)
Using 6mm (US size J/10) hook and B, make a magic ring.
Round 1: 5dc in ring. *5 sts.*
Work in a continuous spiral. PM in last st and move up as each round is finished.
Round 2: 2dc in each st to end. *10 sts.*
Round 3: [1dc in next st, 2dc in next st] 5 times. *15 sts.*
Round 4: [1dc in each of next 2 sts, 2dc in next st] 5 times. *20 sts.*
Round 5: *Ch6, sl st in second ch from hook, 1dc in next ch, 1htr in next ch, 1tr in next ch, 1dtr in next ch, miss 3 sts on central circle, sl st in next st; rep from * 4 times to make 5 points in total, sl st in base of first point to join.
Fasten off.

TIP

As the main yarn is quite bulky, when finishing off your ends you may find it easier to use a small crochet hook to pull all the ends to the inside of the basket and tie them off. Loose ends can then be woven underneath the inside stitches with a crochet hook.

Making up and finishing

With the RS of the base facing down, fold the four sides of the basket up and pin together with large pins or safety pins. Work a dc seam down each of the four corners. Fasten off.

Thread the handle ends through from the outside to the inside of the basket, approximately one row down and six stitches apart, on opposite sides of the basket. Tie a large knot at each end to hold the handle in place.

Using a sewing needle and thread, stitch one star onto the centre of each side.

Using 6mm (US size J/10) hook and B, work 2dc in each st around the top edge. Fasten off. Sew in any ends.

BOBBLY RECTANGULAR CUSHION

With the sharp contrast of the white bobbles against the mustard background, this cushion will add an instant splash of sunshine brightness to any sofa or armchair. The ruffle edging finishes off the sides nicely.

SKILL LEVEL ● ●

YARN AND MATERIALS

Cascade Yarns Spuntaneous Worsted (100% wool, 190m/208yd per 100g/3½oz ball) aran (worsted) weight yarn:
  3 balls of Gold shade 07 (A)

Debbie Bliss Baby Cashmerino (55% wool, 33% acrylic, 12% cashmere, 125m/137yd per 50g/1¾oz ball) 5-ply (sport) weight yarn:
  1 ball of White shade 100 (B)

42 x 30cm (16½x 12in) cushion pad

3 snap fasteners

3 buttons

HOOKS AND EQUIPMENT

4.5mm (US size 7) crochet hook

Pins

Sewing needle and thread

FINISHED MEASUREMENTS

Width 42cm (16½in), height 30cm (12in)

TENSION (GAUGE)

15 sts x 15 rows = 8.5 x 7.5cm (3¼ x 3in) working double crochet, using a 4.5mm (US size 7) crochet hook and Cascade Yarns Spuntaneous Worsted.

ABBREVIATIONS

See page 127.

SPECIAL ABBREVIATION

MB (make bobble): using yarn that is laid along top of row, [yarn round hook, insert hook in stitch, yarn round hook, pull yarn through work, yarn round hook, pull yarn through first 2 loops on hook] 6 times all in same stitch, using main colour yarn round hook, pull through all loops on hook

Cushion cover

Using 4.5mm (US size 7) hook and A, ch72.

Row 1 (RS): 1dc in second ch from hook, 1dc in each ch to end, turn. *71 sts.*

Rows 2–12: Ch1 (does not count as st throughout), 1dc in each st to end, turn.

Row 13 (bobble row 1): Ch1, lay B along top of row as you work, using A, 1dc in each of next 5 sts, [using B, MB, using A, 1dc in each of next 11 sts] 5 times, using B, MB, using A, 1dc in each of next 5 sts.

Rows 14–22: Ch1, 1dc in each st to end.

Row 23 (bobble row 2): Ch1, lay B along top of row as you work, using A, 1dc in each of next 11 sts, [using B, MB, using A, 1dc in each of next 11 sts] 5 times.

Rows 24–32: As Rows 14–22.

Rep Rows 13–32 until work measures 63cm (25in), ending with a RS row.

BORDER

Round 1: Work a second dc in last st of prev row (corner made), work 1dc in each row end down left-hand side, 2dc in corner st, work 1dc in each st along bottom edge, 2dc in corner st, work 1dc in each row end up right-hand side of cushion, 2dc in corner st, sl st in top of first st of last row of cushion to join.

Fasten off.

Making up and finishing

Lay the cushion cover on a flat surface, RS down. Place the cushion pad in the middle, fold the bottom of the cover up and the top of the cover down so that the cushion pad is enclosed, and the two edges overlap. Pin across the join at the back of the cushion where the opening will be. Pin the sides.

RUFFLE EDGE

Row 1: Using 4.5mm (US size 7) hook and A, work a dc seam to join layers down one side, do not fasten off, turn.

Row 2: Ch1 (does not count as st throughout), 2dc in each st to end, turn.

Row 3: Ch1, 2dc in each st to end.

Fasten off.

Rep on other side of cushion.

Sew in any ends.

Stitch the three snap fasteners into place so that the opening of the cushion is closed, and the fasteners are hidden underneath the overlapping flap. Using a sewing needle and thread, sew the three buttons onto the back of the cushion, directly above where the fasteners are.

CHAPTER 4

KITCHEN & DINING

SHAKER BIRDHOUSE CUSHION

Popped on a chair in the corner of your kitchen, this cushion helps to create the perfect little cosy corner for those cup of tea and feet up moments. Worked in cotton and removable, the cover is fully washable.

SKILL LEVEL ● ●

YARN AND MATERIALS

Cascade Ultra Pima (100% cotton, 200m/219yd per 100g/3½oz ball) DK (light worsted) weight yarn:
  4 balls of Natural shade 3718 (A)

Drops Cotton Merino (50% Cotton, 50% Wool, 110m/120yd per 50g/1¾oz ball) DK (light worsted) weight yarn:
  1 ball each of:
  Beige shade 03 (B)
  Mustard Yellow shade 15 (C)
  Pistachio shade 10 (D)
  Powder Pink shade 05 (E)
  Sea Green shade 29 (F)

5mm (¼in) safety eye or black embroidery thread

40 x 40cm (16 x 16in) cushion pad

75cm (30in) of cord for bunting

1m (1yd) of pompom edging

3 snap fasteners

3 coordinating buttons

HOOKS AND EQUIPMENT

4mm (US size G/6) crochet hook

3mm (US size C/2–D/3) crochet hook

Yarn needle

Stitch marker

Safety pins

Piece of cardboard same size as cushion pad

Sewing needle and thread

FINISHED MEASUREMENTS

Width 40cm (16in), length 40cm (16in)

TENSION (GAUGE)

15 sts x 15 rows = 7.5 x 7cm (3 x 2¾in) working double crochet, using a 4mm (US size G/6) crochet hook with A.

ABBREVIATIONS

See page 127.

Cushion cover

Using 4mm (US size G/6) hook and A, ch81.
Row 1: 1dc in second ch from hook, 1dc in each ch to end, turn. *80 sts.*
Row 2: Ch1, 1dc in each of next 80 sts, turn.
Rep Row 2 until work measures 86cm (34in), ending with a RS row. Do not fasten off.

BORDER

Work a second dc in last st of row (corner made), work 1dc in each row end down left-hand side, 2dc in corner st, work 1dc in each st along bottom edge, 2dc in corner st, work 1dc in each row end up right-hand side of cushion, 2dc in corner st, sl st in first st of last row of cushion to join.
Fasten off.

EDGES

With RS of cover facing you, join D at top of one long edge and work 1dc in each st along edge. Rep on other long edge.
Fasten off.

Birdhouse

(make 1)
Using 3mm (US size C/2–D/3) hook and B, ch18.
Row 1: 1dc in second ch from hook, 1dc in each ch to end. *17 sts.*
Turn at end of this and every foll row.
Row 2: Ch1 (does not count as st throughout), 2dc in first st, 1dc in each of next 15 sts, 2dc in last st. *19 sts.*
Rows 3–4: Ch1, 1dc in each st to end.
Row 5: Ch1, 2dc in first st, 1dc in each of next 17 sts, 2dc in last st. *21 sts.*
Rows 6–9: Ch1, 1dc in each st to end.
Row 10: Ch1, 2dc in first st, 1dc in each of next 19 sts, 2dc in last st. *23 sts.*
Rows 11–16: Ch1, 1dc in each st to end.
Row 17: Ch1, 2dc in first st, 1dc in each of next 21 sts, 2dc in last st. *25 sts.*
Rows 18–21: Ch1, 1dc in each st to end.
Row 22: Ch1, dc2tog, 1dc in each of next 21 sts, dc2tog. *23 sts.*
Row 23: Ch1, dc2tog, 1dc in each of next 19 sts, dc2tog. *21 sts.*

Row 24: Ch1, dc2tog, 1dc in each of next 17 sts, dc2tog. *19 sts.*
Row 25: Ch1, dc2tog, 1dc in each of next 15 sts, dc2tog. *17 sts.*
Row 26: Ch1, dc2tog, 1dc in each of next 13 sts, dc2tog. *15 sts.*
Row 27: Ch1, dc2tog, 1dc in each of next 11 sts, dc2tog. *13 sts.*
Row 28: Ch1, dc2tog, 1dc in each of next 9 sts, dc2tog. *11 sts.*
Row 29: Ch1, dc2tog, 1dc in each of next 7 sts, dc2tog. *9 sts.*
Row 30: Ch1, dc2tog, 1dc in each of next 5 sts, dc2tog. *7 sts.*
Row 31: Ch1, dc2tog, 1dc in each of next 3 sts, dc2tog. *5 sts.*
Row 32: Ch1, dc2tog, 1dc in next st, dc2tog. *3 sts.*
Row 33: Ch1, dc2tog, 1dc in next st. *2 sts.*
Row 34: Ch1, dc2tog.
Fasten off.
With RS facing, using 3mm (US size C/2–D/3) hook, join C with a sl st at left-hand side of Row 21, ch1 and work 1dc in each row end down left hand side wall, 3dc in corner st, work 1dc in each st along bottom edge, 3dc in corner st, work 1dc in each row end up right-hand side wall, ending at right-hand side of Row 21.
Fasten off.

Birdhouse roof side one

(make 1)
Using 3mm (US size C/2–D/3) hook and C, ch26.
Row 1: Dc2tog across second and third ch from hook, 1dc in each of next 22 ch, 2dc in last ch. *25 sts.*
Turn at end of this and every foll row.
Row 2: Ch1 (does not count as st throughout), 2dc in first st, 1dc in each of next 22 sts, dc2tog.
Row 3: Ch1, dc2tog, 1dc in each of next 22 sts, 2dc in last st.
Row 4: Ch1, 2dc in first st, 1dc in each of next 22 sts, dc2tog.
Row 5: Ch1, dc2tog, 1dc in each of next 22 sts, 2dc in last st.
Do not fasten off, do not turn.

EDGING
At end of Row 5, ch1, work 1dc in each row end down short, slanted edge, 2dc in corner st, work 1dc in each st along bottom edge, 2dc in corner st, work 1dc in each row end up short, slanted edge, sl st in first st of row to join.
Fasten off.

Birdhouse roof side two

(make 1)
Using 3mm (US size C/2–D/3) hook and C, ch26.
Row 1: 2dc in second ch from hook, 1dc in each of next 22 ch, dc2tog across last 2 ch. *25 sts.*
Turn at end of this and every foll row.
Row 2: Ch1 (does not count as st throughout), dc2tog, 1dc in each of next 22 sts, 2dc in last st.
Row 3: Ch1, 2dc in first st, 1dc in each of next 22 sts, dc2tog.
Row 4: Ch1, dc2tog, 1dc in each of next 22 sts, 2dc in the last st.
Row 5: Ch1, 2dc in first st, 1dc in each of next 22 sts, dc2tog.
Do not fasten off, do not turn.

EDGING
At end of Row 5, ch1, work 1dc in each row end down short, slanted edge, 2dc in corner st, work 1dc in each st along bottom edge, 2dc in corner st, work 1dc in each row end up short, slanted edge, sl st in first st of row to join.
Fasten off.

Birdhouse door

(make 1)
Using 3mm (US size C/2–D/3) hook and E, make a magic ring.
Round 1: 6dc in ring, sl st in top of first dc to join. *6 sts.*
Work in a continuous spiral. PM in last st and move up as each round is finished.
Round 2: [2dc in next st] 6 times. *12 sts.*
Round 3: [1dc in next st, 2dc in next st] 6 times. *18 sts.*
Round 4: 1dc in next st, 2dc in next st, [1dc in each of next 2 sts, 2dc in next st] 5 times, 1dc in last st. *24 sts.*
Round 5: [1dc in each of next 3 sts, 2dc in next st] 6 times, sl st in first dc to join. *30 sts.*
Fasten off.
Round 6: Join F with a sl st in any st, working in back loops only, sl st loosely in each st around door edge, sl st in first sl st to join.
Fasten off.

Bunting

(make 2 each in C, E and F)
Using 3mm (US size C/2–D/3) hook and either C, E or F, ch10.
Row 1: 1dc in second ch from hook, 1dc in each ch to end. *9 sts.*
Turn at end of this and every foll row.

Row 2: Ch1 (does not count as st throughout), 1dc in each st to end.

Row 3: Ch1, dc2tog, 1dc in each of next 5 sts, dc2tog. *7 sts.*

Row 4: Ch1, 1dc in each st to end.

Row 5: Ch1, dc2tog, 1dc in each of next 3 sts, dc2tog. *5 sts.*

Row 6: Ch1, 1dc in each st to end.

Row 7: Ch1, dc2tog, 1dc in next st, dc2tog. *3 sts.*

Row 8: Ch1, 1dc in each st to end.

Row 9: Ch1, dc2tog, 1dc in next st, dc2tog. *2 sts.*

Row 10: Ch1, dc2tog.

Turn, so RS of flag is facing you, ch1 and work 1dc in each st and row end around flag edge, working 2dc in each corner st, sl st in top of ch-1 to join. Fasten off.

Bird

(make 1)

Using 3mm (US size C/2–D/3) hook and F, ch6.

Row 1: 2dc in second ch from hook, 1dc in each ch to last ch, 2dc in last ch. *7 sts.*

Turn at end of this and every foll row.

Row 2: Ch1 (does not count as st throughout), 2dc in first st, 1dc in each of next 5 sts, 2dc in last st. *9 sts.*

Rows 3–8: Ch1, 2dc in next st, 1dc in each st to last st, 2dc in last st. *21 sts at end of Row 8.*

Row 9: Ch1, 1dc in each of next 20 sts, 2dc in last st. *22 sts.*

Row 10: Ch1, 1dc in each of next 20 sts, dc2tog. *21 sts.*

Row 11: Ch1, dc2tog, 1dc in each of next 17 sts, dc2tog. *19 sts.*

Row 12: Ch1, 1dc in each of next 17 dc, dc2tog. *18 sts.*

Row 13: Ch1, sl st in first st, 1dc in each of next 15 dc, dc2tog.

Row 14: Ch1, 1dc in each of next 8 sts, sl st in next st and turn, leaving remaining sts unworked. *8 sts.*

Row 15: Ch1, miss sl st, 1dc in each of next 8 sts. *8 sts.*

Row 16: Ch1, 2dc in next st, 1dc in each of next 6 sts, sl st in last st.

Row 17: Ch1, miss sl st, 1dc in each of next 7 sts, 2dc in last st. *9 sts.*

Row 18: Ch1, dc2tog, 1dc in each of next 6 sts, sl st in last st. *7 sts.*
Row 19: Ch1, miss sl st, dc2tog, 1dc in each of next 3 sts, dc2tog. *5 sts.*
Row 20: Ch1, 1dc in each of next 3 sts, dc2tog. *4 sts.*
Row 21: Ch1, 1dc in each of next 2 st, dc2tog. *3 sts.*
Row 22: Ch1, dc2tog, sl st in last st.
Fasten off.
With RS facing, join F at top of head with a sl st, ch1 and work dc evenly down back of head and along curve of neck, sl st in each st along bird's back, work 6dc across tail, sl st in each row end and st along bird's underbelly and up side of neck, work dc evenly around front of head, sl st in top of ch-1 to join.
Fasten off.

TAIL

Using 3mm (US size C/2–D/3) hook and F, rejoin yarn at start of tail with a sl st in back loop only of first of six tail dc, *ch8, 1htr in second ch from hook, 1htr in each of next 4 ch, 1dc in each of next 2 ch, sl st in back loop only of second tail st; rep from * to make 4 more tail feathers.
Fasten off.

BEAK

(make 1)
Using 3mm (US size C/2–D/3) hook and C, ch4.
Row 1: 1dc in second ch from hook, 1dc in each of next 2 sts, turn. *3 sts*
Row 2: Ch1, 1dc in each st to end, turn.
Row 3: Ch1, dc3tog.
Fasten off.

WING

(make 1)
Using 3mm (US size C/2–D/3) hook and B, ch6.
Row 1: 1dc in second ch from hook, 1dc in each ch to end. *5 sts.*
Turn at end of this and every foll row.
Row 2: Ch1 (does not count as st throughout), 2dc in first st, 1dc in each of next 3 sts, 2dc in the last st. *7 sts.*
Rows 3–4: Ch1, 1dc in each st to end.
Row 5: Ch1, 2dc in first st, 1dc in each of next 5 sts, 2dc in last st. *9 sts.*
Rows 6–7: Ch1, 1dc in each st to end.
Row 8: Ch1, dc2tog, 1dc in each of next 5 sts, dc2tog. *7 sts.*
Row 9: Ch1, dc2tog, 1dc in each of next 3 sts, dc2tog. *5 sts.*
Row 10: Ch1, dc2tog, 1dc in next st, dc2tog. *3 sts.*
Row 11: Ch1, 1dc in each of next *3 sts.*
Row 12: Ch1, dc2tog, 1dc in next st. *2 sts.*
Fasten off.
Join F at any point on edge and work 1dc in each st and row end around wing edge, sl st in first dc to join.
Fasten off.

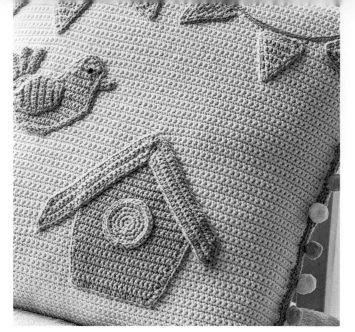

Making up and finishing

Sew in ends.

Stitch the birdhouse door onto the birdhouse. Stitch the wing and beak to the bird. Attach the safety eye or use black embroidery thread to stitch on an eye.

Lay the cushion cover on to a flat surface, RS down. Place the cushion pad in the middle, fold the bottom of the cover up and the top of the cover down so that the cushion pad is enclosed, and the two edges overlap. Pin across the join at the back of the cushion where the opening will be – this will hold the cover in place whilst you position and attach the items to the front of the cushion.

Turn the cushion over so that the RS is facing you. Attach the cord for the bunting along the top of the cushion and fasten in place with a few stitches. Position the birdhouse, bird and bunting where you want them to be. Hold in place with safety pins. Slide the cushion pad out. Slide a piece of cardboard inside to avoid the front and back of the cushion getting stitched together. Using a sewing needle and thread stitch the items securely in place.

Carefully remove the cardboard so as not to lose the shape of the cushion. Cut the piece of pompom edging in half and place a piece on each side of the cushion so that the pompom tape is enclosed between the front and back of the cushion. Pin the sides of the cushion shut so that the front of the cushion, the pompom edging, and the back of the cushion are all held in place. Use a sewing needle and thread to stitch the sides of the cushion securely together.

Stitch the three snap fasteners in to place so that the opening of the cushion is closed, and the fasteners are hidden underneath the overlapping flap. Using a sewing needle and thread sew the three buttons on to the back of the cushion, directly above where the fasteners are.

BEEHIVE TEA COSY

Rather than bees buzzing around the honey pot, with this tea cosy you'll find all the bees will be buzzing around your teapot! Crocheted in simple bobble stitch this cosy is easy to make, with the bees being added after. The cosy is a generous size and will comfortably fit up to a 10-cup teapot.

SKILL LEVEL ● ●

YARN AND MATERIALS

Caron Simply Soft (100% acrylic, 288m/315yd per 170g/6oz ball) aran (worsted) weight yarn:
  2 balls of Bone shade 9703 (A)

Cascade Ultra Pima Fine (100% cotton, 125m/137yd per 50g/1¾oz ball) 5-ply (sport) weight yarn:
  1 ball in each of:
  Yellow Rose shade 3743 (B)
  White shade 3728 (C)

Small amount of 100% polyester toy stuffing

Approx. 20cm (8in) length of cotton tape

HOOKS AND EQUIPMENT

4.5mm (US size 7) crochet hook

2.5mm (US size B/1–C/2) crochet hook

Yarn needle

Stitch marker

Thin black permanent marker

Sewing needle and thread

FINISHED MEASUREMENTS

Width 33cm (13in), depth 22cm (8¾in)
One bee measures approx. 2.5cm (1in) long

TENSION (GAUGE)

15 sts x 15 rows = 8 x 9cm (3¼ x 3½in) working double crochet, using a 4.5mm (US size 7) crochet hook and Caron Simply Soft.

ABBREVIATIONS

See page 127.

SPECIAL ABBREVIATION

MB (make bobble): [yarn round hook, insert hook in stitch, yarn round hook, pull yarn through work, yarn round hook, pull yarn through first 2 loops on hook] 5 times all in same stitch, yarn round hook, pull through all loops on hook

Cosy side

(make 2)
Using 4.5mm (US size 7) hook and A, ch56.
Row 1 (WS): 1dc in second ch from hook, 1dc in each ch to end. *55 sts.*
Turn at end of this and every foll row.
Row 2 (Bobble Row 1): Ch1 (does not count as st throughout), 1dc in each of first 3 sts, *MB in next st, 1dc in each of next 3 sts; rep from * to end. *55 sts.*
Row 3: Ch1, 1dc in each st to end. *55 sts.*
Row 4 (Bobble Row 2): Ch1, 1dc in each of first 5 sts, *MB in next st, 1dc in each of next 3 sts; rep from * to last 2 sts, 1dc in each of last 2 sts. *55 sts.*
Row 5: Ch1, 1dc in each st to end.
Rows 6–25: Rep Rows 2-5 five times.
Row 26: Rep Row 2.
Row 27: Ch1, dc2tog, 1dc in each st to last 2 sts, dc2tog. *53 sts.*
Row 28: Ch1, dc2tog, 1dc in each of next 2 sts, *MB in next st, 1dc in each of next 3 sts; rep from * to last 5 sts, MB in next st, 1dc in each of next 2 sts, dc2tog. *51 sts.*
Row 29: Ch1, dc2tog, 1dc in each st to last 2 sts, dc2tog. *49 sts.*

Row 30: Ch1, dc2tog, 1dc in each of next 2 sts, *MB in next st, 1dc in each of next 3 sts; rep from * to last 5 sts, MB in next st, 1dc in each of next 2 sts, dc2tog. *47 sts.*
Row 31: Ch1, dc2tog, 1dc in each st to last 2 sts, dc2tog. *45 sts.*
Row 32: Ch1, dc2tog, 1dc in each of next 2 sts, *MB in next st, 1dc in each of next 3 sts; rep from * to last 5 sts, MB in next st, 1dc in each of next 2 sts, dc2tog. *43 sts.*
Row 33: Ch1, dc2tog, 1dc in each st to last 2 sts, dc2tog. *41 sts.*
Row 34: Ch1, dc2tog, 1dc in each of next 2 sts, *MB in next st, 1dc in each of next 3 sts; rep from * to last 5 sts, MB in next st, 1dc in each of next 2 sts, dc2tog. *39 sts.*
Row 35: Ch1, dc2tog, 1dc in each st to last 2 sts, dc2tog. *37 sts.*
Row 36: Ch1, dc2tog, 1dc in each of next 2 sts, *MB in next st, 1dc in each of next 3 sts; rep from * to last 5 sts, MB in next st, 1dc in each of next 2 sts, dc2tog. *35 sts.*
Row 37: Ch1, dc2tog, 1dc in each st to last 2 sts, dc2tog. *33 sts.*
Row 38: Ch1, dc2tog, 1dc in each of next 2 sts, *MB in next st, 1dc in each of next 3 sts; rep from * to last 5 sts, MB in next st, 1dc in each of next 2 sts, dc2tog. *31 sts.*
Row 39: Ch1, dc2tog, 1dc in each st to last 2 sts, dc2tog. *29 sts.*
Row 40: Ch1, dc2tog, 1dc in each of next 2 sts, *MB in next st, 1dc in each of next 3 sts; rep from * to last 5 sts, MB in next st, 1dc in each of next 2 sts, dc2tog. *27 sts.*
Row 41: Ch1, [dc2tog] 13 times, sl st in last st. *13 sts.*
Row 42: Ch1, [dc2tog] 6 times, sl st in last st.
Fasten off.

Bees

(make 20)
Using 2.5mm (US size B/1–C/2) hook and B, make a magic ring.
Round 1: 4dc into the ring. *4 sts.*
Work in a continuous spiral. PM in last st and move up as each round is finished.
Round 2: [1dc in first st, 2dc in next st] twice. *6 sts.*
Round 3: [1dc in each of next 2 sts, 2dc in next st] twice. *8 sts.*
Rounds 4–6: 1dc in each st to end.
Fill the bee with a tiny amount of stuffing.
Round 7: [Dc2tog] 4 times. *4 sts.*
Fasten off, using yarn end to sew hole closed.

Wings

(make 1 per bee)
Using 2.5mm (US size B/1–C/2) hook and C, ch2.
Work ([1dc, 1htr, 2tr, 1htr, 1dc] twice) in second ch from hook.
Fasten off, leaving a long yarn tail.

Making up and finishing

BEES

Using the black pen mark a few stripes around each bee's body and mark two black dots for the eyes.
Fold each wing in half to make two semicircles. Attach a wing to the back of each bee by threading the white yarn tails down through to the underside of the bee and secure underneath. Do not cut the yarn ends.

COSY

With RS facing, stitch the two sides of the cosy together. Turn RS out.

Thread a short piece of cotton tape through the centre top of the cosy to create a hanging loop, and sew in place with needle and thread.

Attach the bees randomly over the cosy by threading the yarn tails through to the inside of the cosy and tying securely with a knot on the inside.

WAFFLE STITCH TABLE MATS

Crocheted in waffle stitch, these table mats work up to give a lovely, thick, textured protector to use on your dining table. Edged in crab stitch in a contrast colour they can be personalised to match your plates. The yarn used in this pattern is 100% cotton and fully washable.

SKILL LEVEL ● ●

YARN AND MATERIALS

For one tablemat:

Cascade Ultra Pima (100% cotton, 200m/219yd per 100g/3½oz ball) DK (light worsted) weight yarn:
  1 ball of Sage shade 3720 (A)

Cascade Yarns Noble Cotton (100% cotton, 201m/220yd per 100g/3½oz ball) DK (light worsted) weight yarn:
  Small amount of Pale Gold shade 15 (B)

HOOKS AND EQUIPMENT

3.5mm (US size E/4) crochet hook

3mm (US size C/2–D/3) crochet hook

Yarn needle

FINISHED MEASUREMENTS

Width 31cm (12¼in), length 22cm (8¾in)

TENSION (GAUGE)

14 sts x 6 rows = 6 x 5cm (2⅜ x 2in) working waffle stitch, using a 3.5mm (US size E/4) crochet hook and Cascade Ultra Pima.
15 sts x 15 rows = 6.5 x 7cm (2½ x 2¾in) working double crochet using a 3mm (US size C/2–D/3) crochet hook and Cascade Yarns Noble Cotton.

ABBREVIATIONS

See page 127.

SPECIAL ABBREVIATION

FPtr (front post treble): yarn round hook, from front of work insert hook from right to left behind post of next st on prev round and through to front again, yarn round hook and pull loop through, [yarn round hook, draw through 2 loops] twice

Table mat

Using 3.5mm (US size E/4) crochet hook and A, ch70.
Row 1 (WS): 1tr in third ch from hook, 1tr in each ch to end, turn. *68 sts.*
Row 2: Ch1 (does not count as st throughout), 1tr in each of first 2 sts, *1FPtr in next st, 1tr in each of next 2 sts; rep from * to end, turn.
Row 3: Ch1, 1tr in first st, 1FPtr in next st, 1tr in next st, *1FPtr in each of next 2 sts, 1tr in next st; rep from * to last 2 sts, 1FPtr in next st, 1tr in last st, turn.
Rep Rows 2 and 3 thirteen times.
Rep Row 2 once more.
Fasten off.

BORDER

Round 1: With RS facing join in A in bottom right-hand corner, 1dc in each row end up right-hand side, 2dc in corner st, 1dc in each st across top edge, 2dc in corner st, 1dc in each row end down to bottom left-hand corner, 1dc in each st across bottom edge, 2dc in corner st, sl st in top of first dc to join.
Round 2: Ch1, work crab stitch around mat as follows: working clockwise with RS facing, [inserting hook from back to front, work 1dc in next st to right] to end of round, sl st in top of ch-1 to join.
Fasten off.

Making up and finishing

Using 3mm (US size C/2–D/3) hook and B, work 2 rounds of sl st working from the top of the table mat through to the bottom, the first round being just under the crab stitch and the second round being on the inside of first border round. Fasten off and sew in any ends.

> **TIP**
>
> Working one chain, rather than two, at the start of each row keeps the edges straight and neat.

WASHING LINE PEG BAG

Chase those rainy-day blues away with this fun peg bag – it may even make hanging out the washing an absolute joy!

YARN AND MATERIALS

Cascade Ultra Pima (100% cotton, 200m/219yd per 100g/3½oz ball) DK (light worsted) weight yarn:
  2 balls of Sage shade 3720 (A)

Rowan Summerlite 4-ply (100% cotton, approx. 175m/191yd per 50g/1¾oz ball), 4-ply (fingering) weight yarn:
  1 ball in each of:
  High Tide shade 428 (B)
  Touch of Gold shade 439 (C)
  Langoustine shade 440 (D)

1 wooden hanger, cut to 26cm (10¼in) width

14 mini wooden clothes pegs, 25mm (1in) long

1m (1yd) string

HOOKS AND EQUIPMENT

4mm (US size G/6) crochet hook

3mm (US size C/2–D/3) crochet hook

2.5mm (US size B/1–C/2) crochet hook

Yarn needle

Sewing needle and thread

FINISHED MEASUREMENTS

Width 28cm (11in), length 25cm (10in)

TENSION (GAUGE)

15 sts x 15 rows = 7.5 x 6.5cm (3 x 2½in) working double crochet, using a 4mm (US size G/6) crochet hook and Cascade Ultra Pima.
15 sts x 15 rows = 6cm (2⅜in) square working double crochet, using a 2.5mm (US size B/1–C/2) crochet hook and Rowan Summerlite 4-ply.

ABBREVIATIONS

See page 127.

Peg bag

Using 4mm (US size G/6) hook and A, ch51.
Row 1: 1dc in second ch from hook, 1dc in each ch to end, turn. *50 sts.*
Row 2: Ch1 (does not count as st), 1dc in each st to end, turn.
Rep Row 2 until work measures 52cm (20½in), ending with RS facing. Do not turn and do not fasten off A at end of last row.

EDGING

Work a second dc in final st of prev row, then work 1dc in each row end down left-hand side, 2dc in corner st, 1dc in each st along bottom edge, 2dc in corner st, 1dc in each row end up right-hand side, sl st in top of first dc of prev row to join.
Fasten off.

Shorts

(make 1 pair in B, 1 pair in D)
Using 2.5mm (US size B/1–C/2) hook, ch23.
Row 1: 1dc in second ch from hook, 1dc in each ch to end, turn. *22 sts.*
Rows 2–6: Ch1 (does not count as st throughout), 1dc in each st to end, turn.
Row 7: Ch1, 1dc in each of first 11 sts, turn. *11 sts.*
Rows 8–11: Ch1, 1dc in each of next 11 sts, turn.
Row 12: Ch1, 2dc in first st, 1dc in each st to last st, 2dc in last st. *13 sts.*
Fasten off.
With RS facing re-join yarn to rem 11 sts at Row 7 and rep Rows 7–12 to complete second leg.
Fasten off.

ADD DECORATION

With RS of shorts in B facing, using 2.5mm (US size B/1–C/2) hook and C, working just below top row (Row 1) of shorts, sl st from top of shorts through to bottom to make belt.
Fasten off.
Using yarn needle and C, stitch a square in centre of belt for buckle.
With RS of shorts in D facing, using 2.5mm (US size B/1–C/2) hook and C, work sl st to create stripes from top of shorts down to bottom of each leg.
Fasten off.

Socks

(make 3 pairs, 1 each in B, C and D)
Using 2.5mm (US size B/1–C/2) hook and B, C or D,
ch10.
Row 1: Dc2tog in second and third ch from hook, 1dc
in each of next 7 ch, turn. *8 sts.*
Row 2: Ch1 (does not count as st throughout), 1dc in
each st to end, turn. *8 sts.*
Row 3: Do not ch1, miss first dc, dc2tog, 1dc in each
of last 5 sts, turn. *6 sts.*
Row 4: Ch1, 1dc in each of first 4 sts, turn. *4 sts.*
Rows 5–8: Ch1, 1dc in each of next *4 sts.*
Sl st in each st and row end around edge of sock.
Fasten off

ADD DECORATION
With RS of socks in C facing, using B, oversew cuff
and heel.
With RS of socks in B facing, using D, stitch French
knots across sock and oversew cuff.
With RS of socks in D facing, using C, work short
stitches across sock and add ruffle along cuff by using

2.5mm (US size B/1–C/2) hook to work 2dc in each st
along top edge.
Fasten off.

Skirt

Using 2.5mm (US size B/1–C/2) hook and C, ch20.
Row 1: 1dc in second ch from hook, 1dc in each ch to
end, turn. *19 sts.*
Rows 2–4: Ch1 (does not count as st), 1dc in each st
to end, turn.
Row 5: Ch2 (does not count as st throughout), 2tr in
each st to end, turn. *38 sts.*
Row 6: Ch2, 2tr in each st to end. *76 sts.*
Fasten off.

ADD DECORATION
Using yarn needle and B, oversew along top edge
of skirt.
Fasten off.
Using B, sew French knots along bottom edge of skirt.

Top

Using 2.5mm (US size B/1–C/2) hook and C, ch13.
Row 1 (RS): 1dc in second ch from hook, 1dc in each ch to end, turn. *12 sts.*
Row 2: Ch1 (does not count as st throughout), 1dc in each st to end, turn.
Rows 3–10: Rep Row 2.
Row 11: Ch1, 1dc in each of first 3 sts, ch7, miss next 6 sts, 1dc in each of last 3 sts, turn. *6 sts.*
Row 12: Ch1, 1dc in each of first 3 sts, 6dc along ch-7 from prev row, 1dc in each of last 3 sts, turn. *12 sts.*
Rows 13–21: Ch1, 1dc in each st to end.
Fasten off.

SLEEVES

Using 2.5mm (US size B/1–C/2) hook and with RS facing, join C to side edge of top at Row 7.
Row 1 (RS): Work 1dc in each row end of Rows 7–16, turn. *10 sts.*
Rows 2–5: Ch1, 1dc in each st to end, turn.
Fasten off.
With RS facing using 2.5mm (US size B/1–C/2) hook, join C to side edge of top at Row 16.
Row 1 (RS): Work 1dc in each row end of Rows 16-7, turn. *10 sts.*
Rows 2–5: Ch1, 1dc in each st to end, turn.
Fasten off.

ADD DECORATION

Using yarn needle and B, oversew around neck, bottom of sleeves and bottom of top. Stitch a star shape at centre front.

Making up and finishing

Lay the peg bag on a flat surface, RS down. Fold down 8cm (3⅛in) at the top and fold up 18cm (7⅛in) at the bottom. Pin in place down both sides.

Using the 4mm (US size G/6) hook and 2 strands of B, join each of the two sides of the peg bag with a dc seam.
Fasten off.

EDGING

Using 4mm (US size G/6) hook re-join 2 strands of B at top of one side seam with ch1.
Row 1: Sl st in first st, miss next st, *3htr in next st, miss next st, 1sl st in next st; rep from * to bottom edge (note you may not end with full rep).
Fasten off.
Rep on other side.

Insert the hanger into the peg bag through the front opening, bringing the hook out at the centre of the top edge. Using 3mm (US size C/2–D/3) hook and 2 strands of B, work double crochet all round the hook of the peg bag.
Fasten off.

Using a yarn needle and A, oversew the joining edges at the front opening together, keeping the joining seam as flat as possible and leaving an opening 13cm (5in) wide in the centre.

Using 3mm (US size C/2–D/3) hook and 2 strands of B, sl st in each st around the edge of the centre opening.

Using 3mm (US size C/2–D/3) hook and 2 strands of B, work double crochet all round the hook of the peg bag.
Fasten off.

CLOTHING

To sew the shorts together, lay one pair RS down and fold each leg in half lengthways so that they meet at centre back. Stitch in place. Rep on second pair.
To sew the skirt together, lay RS down and fold each side in to join at centre back. Stitch in place.

To sew the top together, lay RS down and fold over at the neckline. Stitch in place down each side and along the bottom of each sleeve.

Cut two lengths of string and thread into the peg bag to create two washing lines, one above the opening and one below. Secure with chunky knots at each end. Hang the items of clothing on the washing line with the wooden pegs, adding a few holding stitches with a sewing needle and thread where needed.

NESTING BIRD TEA COSY

This quirky and fun tea cosy gives off the homeliest of vibes, with a little bird having chosen to make his nest right on the top! The cosy is made to fit a 10-cup teapot and is generous in fit.

SKILL LEVEL ● ●

YARN AND MATERIALS

Caron Simply Soft (100% acrylic, 288m/315yd per 170g/6oz ball) aran (worsted) weight yarn:
  2 balls of Bone shade 9703 (A)

Drops Cotton Merino (50% cotton, 50% wool, 110m/120yd per 50g/1¾oz ball) DK (light worsted) weight yarn:
  1 ball each of
  Mustard Yellow shade 15 (B)
  Beige shade 03 (C)
  Small amount of Off White shade 01 (D)

Cascade Ultra Pima (100% cotton, 200m/219yd per 100g/3½oz ball) DK (light worsted) weight yarn:
  1 ball each of:
  Spring Green shade 3762 (E)
  Sprout shade 3740 (F)

Small amount of 100% polyester toy stuffing

Black embroidery thread

Dark green sewing thread

A few artificial ivy leaves (optional)

Small twigs

HOOKS AND EQUIPMENT

5mm (US size H/8) crochet hook

4mm (US size G/6) crochet hook

3mm (US size C/2–D/3) crochet hook

2.5mm (US size B/1–C/2) crochet hook

Locking stitch marker

Yarn needle

Sewing needle and thread

Hot glue gun

FINISHED MEASUREMENTS

Length 23cm (9in), circumference 60cm (23½in)

TENSION (GAUGE)

10 sts x 10 rows = 8.5 x 7.5cm (3¼ x 3in) working double crochet, using a 5mm (US size H/8) crochet hook and 2 strands of Caron Simply Soft held together.

15 sts x 15 rows = 7 x 6cm (2¾ x 2⅜in) working double crochet, using a 3mm (US size C/2-D/3) crochet hook and Cascade Yarns Ultra Pima.

15 sts x 15 rows = 7 x 6.5cm (2¾ x 2½in) working double crochet, using a 3mm (US size C/2-D3) crochet hook and 2 strands of Drops Cotton Merino held together.

ABBREVIATIONS

See page 127.

Tea cosy side

(make 2)
Using 5mm (US size H/8) hook and 2 strands of A held tog, ch35.
Row 1: 1dc in second ch from hook, 1dc in each ch to end, turn. *34 sts.*
Row 2: Ch1 (does not count as st), 1dc BLO in each st to end, turn. *34 sts.*
Rows 3–39: Rep Row 2.
Fasten off.

Nest

(make 1)
Using 4mm (US size G/6) hook and 2 strands of C held tog, make a magic ring.
Round 1: 8dc in ring. *8 sts.*
Work in a continuous spiral. PM in last st and move up as each round is finished.
Round 2: 2dc in each st to end. *16 sts.*
Round 3: *1dc in next st, 2dc in next st; rep from * to end. *24 sts.*

Round 4: *1dc in each of next 2 sts, 2dc in next st; rep from * to end. *32 sts.*
Round 5: *1dc in each of next 3 sts, 2dc in next st; rep from * to end. *40 sts.*
Round 6: *1dc in each of next 4 sts, 2dc in next st; rep from * to end. *48 sts.*
Rounds 7–11: 1dc in each st to end.
Round 12: *1dc in each of next 4 sts, dc2tog; rep from * to end. *40 sts.*
Rounds 13–15: 1dc in each st to end.
Fasten off.

Bird body

(make 1)
Using 3mm (US size C/2–D/3) hook and B, make a magic ring.
Round 1: 6dc in ring. *6 sts.*
Work in a continuous spiral. PM in last st and move up as each round is finished.
Round 2: 2dc in each st to end. *12 sts.*
Round 3: *1dc in next st, 2dc in next st; rep from * to end. *18 sts.*

Rounds 4–6: 1dc in each st to end.
Round 7: 1dc in each of first 10 sts, 2dc in next st, 1dc in each of next 2 sts, 2dc in next st, 1dc in each of last 4 sts. *20 sts.*
Round 8: 1dc in each of first 12 sts, [2dc in next st, 1dc in next st] 4 times. *24 sts.*
Round 9: 1dc in each st to end.
Round 10: 1dc in each of first 15 sts, [2dc in next st, 1dc in each of next 2 sts] 3 times. *27 sts.*
Round 11: 1dc in each of first 14 sts, 2dc in next st, 1dc in each of next 3 sts, 1htr in each of next 5 sts, 1dc in each of next 3 sts, 2dc in last st. *29 sts.*
Round 12: 1dc in each of first 4 sts, dc2tog, 1dc in next st, dc2tog, 1dc in each of next 9 sts, 2dc in next st, 1dc in each of next 2 sts, 2dc in next st, 1dc in each of last 7 sts. *29 sts.*
Round 13: 1dc in each of first 5 sts, dc2tog, 1dc in each of next 5 sts, 2dc in next st, 1dc in each of next 2 sts, 2dc in next st, 1dc in each of next 3 sts, 1htr in next st, 1dc in each of next 2 sts, 2dc in next st, 1dc in each of last 6 sts. *31 sts.*
Round 14: 1dc in each of first 5 sts, [dc2tog] twice, 1dc in each of next 10 sts, 1htr in each of next 6 sts, 1dc in each of last 6 sts. *29 sts.*

Round 15: 1dc in each of first 4 sts, [dc2tog] twice, 1dc in next st, dc2tog, 1dc in each of last 18 sts. *26 sts.*
Round 16: 1dc in each of first 2 sts, [dc2tog] 4 times, 1dc in each of next 5 sts, 1htr in each of next 8 sts, 1dc in each of last 3 sts. *22 sts.*
Round 17: 1dc in each of first 3 sts, [dc2tog] twice. Do not fasten off or turn.
Pinch 2 sides tog along bottom of bird and join with a dc seam across the first 6 sts (working into corresponding sts from both sides). Fasten off, leaving the remaining gap open at the tail end. Lightly stuff head and bottom curve of body.

TAIL

Row 1: Flatten tail end of bird so that the end of the dc seam is at the centre of one side, with top side of tail facing and working into corresponding sts from both sides to join the gap as you go, join in D at right-hand corner of flattened tail, ch1, 1dc in same st as join, 2dc in each of next 2 sts, (1dc, sl st) in next st (left-hand corner of flattened tail). *6 sts.*
Fasten off but do not turn.
Row 2: With top side of tail still facing re-join D at beg of Row 1 with a sl st.

Feather 1: *Ch6, sl st in second ch from hook, sl st in each of next 4 ch, sl st in starting st.

Feather 2: Sl st in next st, ch7, sl st in second ch from hook, sl st in each of next 5 ch, sl st in starting st.

Feathers 3 and 4: Sl st in next st, ch8, sl st in second ch from hook, sl st in each of next 6 ch, sl st in starting st.

Feather 5: As feather 2.

Feather 6: As feather 1.

Fasten off.

Wing 1

Using 3mm (US size C/2–D/3) hook and D, ch7.

Row 1: 1dc in second ch from hook, 1htr in each of next 2 ch, 1tr in each of next 2 ch, (3tr, 1dc) in last ch, working down opposite side of ch, 1dc in each of next 5 ch, join with a sl st in first st.

Fasten off.

Wing 2

Using 3mm (US size C/2–D/3) hook and D, ch7.

Row 1: 1dc in second ch from hook, 1dc in each of next 4 ch, (1dc, 3tr) in last ch, working down opposite side of ch, 1tr in each of next 2 ch, 1htr in each of next 2 ch, 1dc in next ch, join with a sl st in first st.

Fasten off.

Beak

Using 2.5mm (US size B/1–C/2) hook and C, ch2.

Row 1: 2dc in second ch from hook, turn. *2 sts*.

Row 2: Ch1 (does not count as a st throughout), 1dc in first st, 2dc in last st, turn. *3 sts*.

Row 3: Ch1, 2dc in first st, 1dc in next st, 2dc in last st, turn. *5 sts*.

Row 4: Ch1, 2dc in first st, 1dc in each of next 3 sts, 2dc in last st. *7 sts*.

Fasten off, leaving a long tail.

Ivy Leaf

(make 13)

Using 3mm (US size C/2–D/3) hook and E, make a magic ring.

Round 1: 4dc in ring. *4 sts*.

Work in a continuous spiral. PM in last st and move up as each round is finished.

Round 2: 2dc in each st to end. *8 sts*.

Round 3: [1dc in next st, 2dc in next st] 4 times, sl st in first dc to join. *12 sts*.

Point 1: Ch3, sl st in second ch from hook, 1dc in next ch, sl st in next st of central circle.

Point 2: Ch4, sl st in second ch from hook, 1dc in next ch, 1htr in next ch, miss next st of central circle, sl st in next st of central circle.

Point 3: Ch6, sl st in second ch from hook, 1dc in next ch, 1htr in next ch, 1tr in next ch, 1dtr in next ch, miss next 2 sts of central circle, sl st in next st of central circle.

Point 4: Rep Point 2.

Point 5: Rep Point 1.

Sl st in next st of central circle (base of leaf), ch5, sl st in each of next 5 ch, sl st in base of leaf.

Fasten off.

Making up and finishing

To make up the cosy, turn up a 2cm (¾in) hem along the bottom edge of each tea cosy side and stitch into place.

With RS together stitch the side seams as follows:
For the spout side: Stitch 3½cm (1½in) from the bottom edge upwards. Stitch 7½cm (3in) from the top edge down.
For the handle side: Stitch 3cm (1¼in) from the bottom edge upwards. Join 6½cm (2½in) from the top edge down.

To close the top of the cosy, using a yarn needle threaded with a length of A, run a gathering thread all around the top edge of the cosy. Secure the thread tightly as you will be pulling on this quite firmly when gathering up the top. Pull the thread to close the hole and spread the gathers evenly around. Fasten off securely.

IVY DECORATION

Using 3mm (US size C/2–D/3) crochet hook and 2 strands of F held tog, work surface crochet (see page 126) to make the ivy stems. Sew the ivy leaves into position with a needle and sewing thread. Using the dark green sewing thread, stitch veins on the ivy leaves.

BIRD AND NEST

To finish the nest, turn down the top 2.5cm (1in) in to the centre to form a firm edge around. Loosely oversew into place.

To finish the bird, sew on the wings and the beak. Use the black embroidery thread to stitch the eyes.

Sew in any ends. Firmly sew the nest onto the top of the tea cosy, catching the artificial ivy leaves, if used, in place as you stitch. Fill the nest with the small twigs and glue in place with a hot glue gun. Use the glue to stick the bird firmly on top of the twigs.

TEA TOWEL EDGING

To add the prettiest of touches to a tea towel, crochet this simple bobbly edging in cotton yarn along the top and bottom edges of the cloth. This can be worked in any number of colour combinations.

SKILL LEVEL ●

YARN AND MATERIALS

Cascade Ultra Pima (100% cotton, 200m/219yd per 100g/3½oz ball) DK (light worsted) weight yarn:
  1 ball of Sage shade 3720 (A)

Cascade Yarns Noble Cotton (100% cotton, 201m/220yd per 100g/3½oz ball) DK (light worsted) weight yarn:
  1 ball of Pale Gold shade 15 (B)

2 tea towels (any size)

HOOKS AND EQUIPMENT

2.5mm (US size B/1–C/2) crochet hook

Sewing needle with large eye

Yarn needle

FINISHED MEASUREMENTS

Edging: approx. 1.5cm (½in) wide

TENSION (GAUGE)

15 sts x 15 rows = 6.5 x 6cm (2½ x 2⅜in) working double crochet, using a 2.5mm (US size B/1–D/2) crochet hook and Cascade Ultra Pima.

15 sts x 15 rows = 6.5 x 6cm (2½ x 2⅜in) working double crochet, using a 2.5mm (US size B/1–D/2) crochet hook and Cascade Yarns Noble Cotton.

ABBREVIATIONS

See page 127.

SPECIAL ABBREVIATION

MB loop (make bobble loop): [yarn round hook, insert hook in st, yarn round hook, pull through st as if starting a htr, pull loop up to htr height] 5 times all in the same st, leaving all loops on hook, yarn round hook and pull through all loops on hook, ch1

Edging

Using the sewing needle threaded with A or B, sew a line of blanket stitch along the top and bottom edges of the tea towel, spacing stitches approx. 0.5cm (¼in) apart and ending with an even number of sts.

Using a 2.5mm (US size B/1–D/2) hook and A or B, with RS of tea towel facing join yarn at right-hand corner of stitched edge.

Row 1: *1dc in first st, 2dc in next st; rep from * to end of row.
Fasten off first colour.

Row 2: With RS facing, join any colour at right-hand corner, 1dc BLO in each st to end. Fasten off.

Row 3: With RS facing, join any colour at right-hand corner, *sl st BLO in next st, MB loop BLO in next st, sl st BLO in next st; rep from * to end.
Fasten off.

Making up and finishing

Sew in any ends.

> Tip
>
> These would make the perfect Christmas gift if you worked the edging onto a Christmassy tea towel.

CIRCULAR TABLE MATS

These mats are so quick and easy to make that in no time at all you can add a fresh new look to your dining table.

SKILL LEVEL ●

YARN AND MATERIALS

For two mats:
Paintbox Yarns Recycled Ribbon (60% cotton, 40% polyester, 120m/131yd per 250g/8¾oz ball) super chunky (super bulky) weight yarn:
  1 ball of Off White shade 003 (A)

Cascade Yarns Noble Cotton (100% cotton, 201m/220yd per 100g/3½oz ball) DK (light worsted) weight yarn:
  1 ball of Pale Gold shade 15 (B)

HOOKS AND EQUIPMENT

6mm (US size J/10) crochet hook

3.5mm (US size E/4) crochet hook

Stitch marker

Yarn needle

FINISHED MEASUREMENTS

27cm (10½in) diameter

TENSION (GAUGE)

10 sts x 10 rows = 10 x 9.5cm (4 x 3¾in) working double crochet, using a 6mm (US size J/10) crochet hook and Paintbox Yarns Recycled Ribbon.

15 sts x 15 rows = 7 x 6.5cm (2¾ x 2½in) working double crochet, using a 3.5mm (US size E/4) crochet hook and Cascade Yarns Noble Cotton.

ABBREVIATIONS

See page 127.

SPECIAL ABBREVIATION

MB loop (make bobble loop): [yarn round hook, insert hook in st, yarn round hook, pull through st as if starting a htr, pull loop up to htr height] 5 times all in the same st, leaving all loops on hook, yarn round hook and pull through all loops on hook, ch1

Table mat

Using 6mm (US size J/10) hook and A, make a magic ring. Work in a continuous spiral. PM in last st and move up as each round is finished.
Round 1: 6dc in ring. *6 sts.*
Round 2: 2dc in each st to end. *12 sts.*
Round 3: [1dc in next st, 2dc in next st] 6 times. *18 sts.*
Round 4: 1dc in first st, 2dc in next st, [1dc in each of next 2 sts, 2dc in next st] 5 times, 1dc in last st. *24 sts.*
Round 5: [1dc in each of next 3 sts, 2dc in next st] 6 times. *30 sts.*
Round 6: 1dc in each of first 2 sts, 2dc in next st, [1dc in each of next 4 sts, 2dc in next st] 5 times, 1dc in each of last 2 sts. *36 sts.*
Round 7: [1dc in each of next 5 sts, 2dc in next st] 6 times. *42 sts.*
Round 8: 1dc in each of first 3 sts, 2dc in next st, [1dc in each of next 6 sts, 2dc in next st] 5 times, 1dc in each of last 3 sts. *48 sts.*
Round 9: [1dc in each of next 7 sts, 2dc in next st] 6 times. *54 sts.*
Round 10: 1dc in each of first 4 sts, 2dc in next st, [1dc in each of next 8 sts, 2dc in next st] 5 times, 1dc in each of last 4 sts. *60 sts.*
Round 11: [1dc in each of next 9 sts, 2dc in next st] 6 times. *66 sts.*
Round 12: 1dc in each of first 5 sts, 2dc in next st, [1dc in each of next 10 sts, 2dc in next st] 5 times, 1dc in each of last 5 sts. *72 sts.*
Round 13: [1dc in each of next 11 sts, 2dc in next st) 6 times, sl st in top of first dc to join. *78 sts.*
Fasten off.

EDGING
Using 3.5mm (US size E/4) hook, join B in any st.
Round 1: 2dc BLO in each st to end, sl st in top of first dc to join, turn. *156 sts.*
Round 2 (WS): Ch1 (counts as first st), sl st in next st, *MB loop in next st, sl st in each of next 2 sts; rep from * around edge of tablemat, sl st in top of ch-1 to join.
Fasten off.

Making up and finishing

Sew in any ends.

CHAPTER 5

SEASONAL

AUTUMN CUSHION

As the evenings draw in, there is nothing nicer than getting your home cosy for those chillier nights ahead. With this cushion you can add instant autumnal colours to a sofa or armchair.

SKILL LEVEL ● ●

YARN AND MATERIALS

Debbie Bliss Cashmerino Aran (55% merino, 33% acrylic, 12% cashmere, 90m/98yd per 50g/1¾oz ball) aran (worsted) weight yarn:
   7 balls of Beige shade 102 (A)

Rowan Summerlite 4-ply (100% Cotton, 175m/191yds per 50g/1¾oz ball) 4-ply (fingering) weight yarn:
   1 ball each of:
   Langoustino shade 440 (B)
   Ecru shade 436 (C)
   Touch of Gold shade 439 (D)
   Green Bay shade 445 (E)

Small amount of 100% polyester toy stuffing

40 x 30cm (16 x 12in) cushion pad

3 snap fasteners

3 buttons

HOOKS AND EQUIPMENT

4mm (US size G/6) crochet hook

2.5mm (US size B/1–C/2) crochet hook

Yarn needle

Stitch marker

Pins

Safety pins

Piece of cardboard the same size as the cushion pad

Sewing needle and thread

38mm (1½in) pompom maker

FINISHED MEASUREMENTS

Width 40cm (16in), height 30cm (12in)

TENSION (GAUGE)

15 sts x 15 rows = 9 x 7cm (3½ x 2¾in) working double crochet, using a 4mm (US size G/6) crochet hook with A

ABBREVIATIONS

See page 127

Cushion cover

Using 4mm (US size G/6) crochet hook and A, ch71.
Row 1: 1dc in second ch from hook, 1dc in each ch to end, turn. *70 sts.*
Row 2: Ch1, 1dc in each of next 70 sts, turn.
Rep Row 2 until work measures 67cm (26½in), ending with a RS row. Do not fasten off, do not turn.

BORDER
Work a second dc in last st of row (corner made), work 1dc in each row end down left hand side, 2dc in corner st, work 1dc in each st along bottom edge, 2dc in corner st, work 1dc in each row end up right hand side, 2dc in corner st, sl st in first st of last row of cushion to join.
Fasten off.

Acorn cup

(make 2)
Using 2.5mm (US size B/1–C/2) hook and E, make a magic ring.
Round 1: 5dc in ring. *5 sts.*
Work in a continuous spiral. PM in last st and move up as each round is finished.
Round 2: [2dc in next st] 5 times. *10 sts.*
Round 3: [1dc in next st, 2dc in next st] 5 times. *15 sts.*
Round 4: [1dc in each of next 2 sts, 2dc in next st] 5 times. *20 sts.*
Round 5: [1dc in each of next 2 sts, dc2tog] 5 times. *15 sts.*
Fasten off.

Acorn

(make 2)
Using 2.5mm (US size B/1–C/2) hook and C, make a magic ring.
Round 1: 4dc in ring. *4 sts.*
Work in a continuous spiral. PM in last st and move up as each round is finished.
Round 2: [2dc in next st] 4 times. *8 sts.*
Round 3: [1dc in next st, 2dc in next st] 4 times. *12 sts.*
Rounds 4–7: 1dc in each st to end.
Fasten off.

Oak leaves

(make 3 in E and 5 in D)

Using 2.5mm (US size B/1–C/2) hook and E or D, ch14.

Round 1: 1dc in second ch from hook, 1dc in each of next 3 ch, 1htr in each of next 5 ch, 1tr in each of next 3 ch, 5tr in last ch, do not turn, working back down other side of ch, 1tr in each of next 5 ch, 1htr in each of next 4 ch, 1dc in each of next 3 ch, sl st in first st to join. *29 sts.*

Round 2:

Lobe 1: 2dc in first st, sl st in next st, (1dc, 1htr, 1tr) in next st, sl st in next st.

Lobe 2: Sl st in next st, (1dc, 1htr, 1tr) in next st, sl st in next st.

Lobe 3: Sl st in next st, (1dc, 1htr, 2tr) in next st, sl st in next st.

Lobe 4: Sl st in next st, (1dc, 1htr, 2tr) in next st, sl st in next st.

Lobe 5: Sl st in next st, (1dc, 1htr, 1tr) in next st, (1tr, 1htr, 1dc) in next st, sl st in each of next 2 sts.

Lobe 6: Ch2, (1tr, 1htr) in same st as sl st, (1htr, 1dc) in next st, sl st in next st.

Lobe 7: Ch2, (1tr, 1htr, sl st) in next st, sl st in next st.

Lobe 8: Sl st in next st, ch2, (1tr, 1htr) in next st, (1htr, 1dc) in next st, sl st in next st.

Lobe 9: Sl st in next st, ch1, 2htr in next st, 1dc, sl st in next st.

Sl st in base of leaf, ch5, sl st in each of 5 ch, sl st in base of leaf.

Fasten off.

Toadstools

(make 3 in B)

Using 2.5mm (US size B/1–C/2) hook and B, make a magic ring.

Round 1: 6dc in ring. *6 sts.*

Work in a continuous spiral. PM in last st and move up as each round is finished.

Round 2: [1dc in next st, 2dc in the next st] 3 times. *9 sts.*

Round 3: 1dc in each st to end.

Round 4: [1dc in each of next 2 sts, 2dc in next st] 3 times. *12 sts.*

Round 5: 1dc in each st to end.

Round 6: [1dc in each of next 3 sts, 2dc in next st] 3 times. *15 sts.*

Round 7: [1dc in each of next 4 sts, 2dc in next st] 3 times. *18 sts.*

Round 8: [1dc in each of next 5 sts, 2dc in next st] 3 times. *21 sts.*

Fasten off B, join in C.

Round 9: Working in back loops only, 1dc in each st to end. *21 sts.*

Round 10: Working in both loops as usual, 1dc, [dc2tog] 10 times. *11 sts*

Stuff toadstool lightly.

Round 11: [Dc2tog] 6 times, ch14, working back along ch, 1dc in each of next 13 ch, sl st back in base of toadstool.

Fasten off, leaving a long tail.

Making up and finishing

Using the long tail in C and a yarn needle, work French knots (see page 124 all over the top of the toadstool. Fasten off.

Lay the cushion cover on a flat surface, RS down. Place the cushion pad in the middle, fold the bottom of the cover up and the top of the cover down so that the cushion pad is enclosed, and the two edges overlap. Pin across the join at the back of the cushion where the opening will be – this will hold the cover in place whilst you position and attach the acorns, oak leaves and toadstools to the front of the cushion.

Turn the cushion over so that the front of the cushion is facing you and position the acorns, oak leaves and toadstools where you want them to be. Hold in place with safety pins. Slide the cushion pad out. Slide a piece of cardboard inside to avoid the front and back of the cushion getting stitched together. Using a sewing needle and thread stitch the items securely in place.

Carefully remove the cardboard so as not to lose the shape of the cushion and pin the sides of the cushion shut. To join the sides, with the RS of the cushion facing you, using 4mm (US size G/6) hook and A, work a dc seam down each side joining the front and back edges together. Fasten off.

Stitch the three snap fasteners in place so that the opening of the cushion is closed, and the fasteners are hidden underneath the overlapping flap. Using a sewing needle and thread sew the buttons onto the back of the cushion, directly above where the fasteners are.

Using a 38mm (1½in) pompom maker and A, make 14 pompoms, leaving a long tail on the central tie. Position the pompoms, seven down each side of the cushion, and use the long tail to sew them securely in place.

MEADOW CUSHION

With its burst of bright red poppies and the contrasting white of the daisies, this meadow cushion immediately takes to you to a sunny summer's day – perfect for brightening any chair or sofa during the warmer months.

SKILL LEVEL ● ●

YARN AND MATERIALS

Cascade Ultra Pima (100% cotton, 200m/219yd per 100g/3½oz ball) DK (light worsted) weight yarn:
   3 balls of Zen Green shade 3757 (A)
   1 ball each of:
   Wine shade 3713 (B)
   Sprout shade 3740 (C)
   Taupe shade 3759 (D)

Cascade Ultra Pima Fine (100% cotton, 125m/137yd per 50g/1¾oz ball) 5-ply (sport) weight yarn:
   1 ball each of:
   Yellow Rose shade 3743 (E)
   White shade 3728 (F)

40 x 30cm (16 x 12in) cushion pad

3 snap fasteners

3 buttons

HOOKS AND EQUIPMENT

4mm (US size G/6) crochet hook

3mm (US size C/2-D/3) crochet hook

2.5mm (US size B/1–C/2) crochet hook

Yarn needle

Black permanent marker

Piece of cardboard same size as cushion pad

Pins

Safety pins

Sewing needle and thread

FINISHED MEASUREMENTS

Width 42cm (16½in), height 30cm (12in)

TENSION (GAUGE)

15 sts x 15 rows = 7.5 x 6.5cm (3 x 2½in) working double crochet, using a 4mm (US size G/6) crochet hook and Cascade Ultra Pima.

ABBREVIATIONS

See page 127.

Cushion cover

Using 4mm (US size G/6) hook and A, ch81.
Row 1: 1dc in second ch from hook, 1dc in each ch to end, turn. *80 sts*.
Row 2: Ch1 (does not count as st), 1dc in each st to end, turn.
Rep Row 2 until work measures 69cm (27in), ending with a RS row. Do not turn.

EDGING

Work a second dc in last st of row (corner made), work 1dc in each row end down left-hand side, 2dc in corner st, work 1dc in each st along bottom edge, 2dc in corner st, work 1dc in each row end up right-hand side of cushion, 2dc in corner st, sl st in first st of last row of cushion to join.
Fasten off.

Daisy

(make 5)
Using 2.5mm (US size B/1–C/2) hook and E, make a magic ring.
Round 1: 8dc in ring, sl st in top of first dc to join. *8 sts*.
Fasten off E.
Round 2: Join F with a sl st in in any st, *ch5, 1dc in second ch from hook, 1dc in each of next 2 ch, sl st in next ch, sl st in base of ch-5, sl st in next st; rep from * 7 times omitting final sl st on last rep. *8 petals*.
Fasten off.

Poppy

(make 3)
Using 3mm (US size C/2-D/3) hook and B, make a magic ring.
Round 1: 4dc in ring, sl st in top of first dc to join. *4 sts.*
Round 2: Ch1 (does not count as st throughout), 2dc in each st to end, sl st in top of ch-1 to join. *8 sts.*
Round 3: Ch1, *(1dc FLO, 1htr FLO) in next st, (1htr FLO, 1tr FLO, 1dtr FLO) in next st, (1dtr FLO, 1tr FLO, 1htr FLO) in next st, (1htr FLO, 1dc FLO) in next st; rep from * once more, sl st in top of ch-1 to join. *2 petals.*
Fasten off.
Round 4: Join B in back loop of st behind petals of prev round, working into BLO of all sts from prev round, rep Round 3. *2 petals.*
Fasten off.

Large blades of grass

(make 5)
Using 3mm (US size C/2-D/3) hook and C, ch17.
Row 1: Sl st in second ch from hook, 1dc in each ch to end. *16 sts.*
Fasten off.

Small blades of grass

(make 5)
Using 3mm (US size C/2) hook and C, ch12.
Row 1: Sl st in second ch from hook, 1dc in each ch to end. *11 sts.*
Fasten off.

Making up and finishing

Use the permanent black marker to colour the centre of the poppy black.

Lay the cushion cover onto a flat surface, RS down. Place the cushion pad in the middle, fold the bottom of the cover up and the top of the cover down so that the cushion pad is enclosed, and the two edges overlap. Pin across the join at the back of the cushion where the opening will be – this will hold the cover in place whilst you position and attach the flowers and grass to the front of the cushion.

Turn the cushion over so that the front of the cushion is facing you and position the flowers and grass where you want them to be. Hold in place with safety pins. Slide the cushion pad out. Slide a piece of cardboard inside to avoid the front and back of the cushion getting stitched together. Using a sewing needle and thread stitch the flowers and grass securely in place. Using a 3mm (US size C/2-D/3) crochet hook and D, add the poppy stems by working them in surface crochet (see page 126) on the RS of the cover, using the photograph as a guide.

Carefully remove the cardboard so as not to lose the shape of the cushion and pin the sides of the cushion shut.

RUFFLE EDGE
Row 1: Using 4mm (US size G/6) hook and A, work a dc seam to join layers down one side, do not fasten off, turn.
Row 2: Ch1, 2dc in each st to end, turn.
Row 3: Ch1, 2dc in each st to end.
Fasten off.
Rep on other side of cushion.

Sew in any ends. Stitch the three snap fasteners into place so that the opening of the cushion is closed, and the fasteners are hidden underneath the overlapping flap. Using a sewing needle and thread, sew the three buttons onto the back of the cushion, directly above where the fasteners are.

> ### Tip
>
> When working the poppy, at the end of Round 3 turn the flower over, and you will see a circle of eight back loops. For Round 4 you need to work into these back loops, starting in a stitch between the petals of Round 3, so that the new petals will be at a 90-degree angle to the first two petals. You need to work with the RS facing you though, so turn the flower back over before beginning Round 4.

SPRING TABLE RUNNER AND PLACE SETTINGS

There can be nothing more spring-like than fresh green grass and by using a green eyelash yarn you can create a mini lawn to run down the middle of your spring or Easter table. Dotted with primroses, which are made and sewn on separately, it could even make you believe you are having the first picnic of the year!

SKILL LEVEL ● ●

YARN AND MATERIALS

King Cole Moments (100% polyester, 90m/98yd per 50g/1¾oz ball) DK (light worsted) weight yarn:
   5 balls of Sage shade 3037 (A)

Cascade Ultra Pima Fine (100% cotton, 125m/137yds per 50g/1¾oz ball) 5-ply (sport) weight yarn:
   1 ball each of:
   China Pink shade 3711 (B)
   Yellow Rose shade 3743 (C)
   Peridot shade 3825 (D)

HOOKS AND EQUIPMENT

4mm (US size G/6) crochet hook

2.5mm (US size B/1–C/2) crochet hook

Stitch marker

Yarn needle

Water soluble colour pencils in darker shade of yellow and pink

Safety pins

Sewing needle and thread or hot glue gun

FINISHED MEASUREMENTS

Runner: length 75cm (29½in), width 30cm (12in)

Place setting: 8cm (3¼in) square

TENSION (GAUGE)

15 sts x 15 rows = approx. 8 x 8cm (3¼ x 3¼in) working in double crochet, using a 4mm (US size G/6) crochet hook and King Cole Moments.

15 sts x 15 rows = 6 x 5.5cm (2⅜ x 2¼in) working in double crochet, using a 2.5mm (US size B/1–C/2) crochet hook and Cascade Ultra Pima Fine.

ABBREVIATIONS

See page 127.

Table runner

Using 4mm (US size G/6) hook and A, ch61.
Row 1: 1dc in second ch from hook, 1dc in each ch to end, turn. *60 sts.*
Row 2: Ch1 (does not count as st), 1dc in each st to end, turn.
Rep Row 2 until work measures 75cm (29½in).
Fasten off.

Primroses

(make 10 in B and 16 in C)
Using 2.5mm (US size B/1–D/2) hook and B or C, make a magic ring.
Work in a continuous spiral. PM in last st and move up as each round is finished.
Round 1: 5dc in ring. *5 sts.*
Round 2: 2dc in each st to end. *10 sts.*
Round 3: *(Sl st, 1 htr, 1tr, 1dtr) in next st, (1dtr, 1tr, 1htr, sl st) in next st; rep from * 4 more times, sl st in first sl st to join. *5 petals.*
Fasten off.

Large leaf

(make 17)
Using 2.5mm (US size B/1–D/2) hook and D, ch11.
Sl st in second ch from hook, 1dc in next ch, 1htr in next ch, 1tr in next ch, 1dtr in next ch, 1dtr in next ch, 1tr in next ch, 1htr in next ch, 1dc in next ch (sl st, ch1, sl st) in last ch, working down opposite side of ch, 1dc in next ch, 1htr in next ch, 1tr in next ch, 1dtr in next ch, 1dtr in next ch, 1tr in next ch, 1htr in next ch, 1dc in next ch, sl st in last ch.
Fasten off.

Small leaf

(make 18)
Using 2.5mm (US size B/1–D/2) hook and D, ch8.
Sl st in second ch from hook, 1dc in next ch, 1htr in next ch, 1tr in next ch, 1htr in next ch, 1dc in next ch, (sl st, ch1, sl st) in last ch, working down opposite side of ch, 1dc in next ch, 1htr in next ch, 1tr in next ch, 1htr in next ch, 1dc in next ch, sl st in last ch.
Fasten off.

Place settings

(make 4)
Using 4mm (US size G/6) hook and A, ch16.
Row 1: 1dc in second ch from hook, 1dc in each ch to end, turn. *15 sts.*
Rows 2–15: Ch1 (does not count as st), 1dc in each st to end, turn.
Fasten off.

Making up and finishing

Sew in any ends.

Use the soluble colour pencils to colour the centre of each primrose a darker shade.

Lay the runner on a flat surface, RS facing up, and position 22 assorted flowers, 13 large leaves and 14 small leaves where you want them to be. Hold them in place with safety pins. Stitch the decoration onto the runner with a needle and thread, or use a hot glue gun.

Decorate each place setting with one primrose, one small leaf and one large leaf in the same way.

TIP

You could work one of the place settings first to check your tension, since these are the same number of stitches and rows as needed for the tension swatch.

The pattern for this is really simple, but it can be quite tricky to see each stitch when working with eyelash yarn. Check your stitch count every few rows and if need be increase/decrease to keep the stitch count correct. You will find that the fluffiness of the yarn is quite forgiving and when completed you will not notice if some rows have a few more or fewer stitches.

CHRISTMAS CUSHION

With its simple wreath of leaves in shades of green, vivid red holly berries and bright pompom edging, this cushion will certainly give a festive feel to any sofa or armchair. It adds a lovely pop of Christmassy colour.

SKILL LEVEL ● ●

YARN AND MATERIALS

Drops Big Merino (100% merino wool, 75m/82yd per 50g/1¾oz ball) aran (worsted) weight yarn:
   9 balls of Beige shade 19 (A)

Cascade Ultra Pima (100% cotton, 200m/219yd per 100g/3½oz ball) DK (light worsted) weight yarn:
   1 ball each of:
   Sage shade 3720 (B)
   Sprout shade 3740 (C)

Yarn and Colors Must-Have Minis (100% cotton, 25m/27yd per 10g/⅓oz ball) 4-ply (fingering) weight yarn:
   1 ball each of:
   Cardinal shade 031 (D)
   White shade 001 (E)

40 x 40cm (16 x 16in) cushion pad

2m (2yd) of red pompom edging

Approx. 25cm (10in) of 16mm (⅝in) wide red velvet ribbon

3 buttons

3 snap fasteners

HOOKS AND EQUIPMENT

5mm (US size H/8) crochet hook

3.5mm (US size E/4) crochet hook

2.5mm (US size B/1–C/2) crochet hook

Yarn needle

Safety pins

Sewing needle and thread

Piece of cardboard same size as cushion pad

FINISHED MEASUREMENTS

42cm (16½in) square

TENSION (GAUGE)

15 sts x 15 rows = 9 x 7.5cm (3½ x 3in) working double crochet, using a 5mm (US size H/8) crochet hook and Drops Big Merino.

One holly leaf measures approx. 7cm (2¾in) long, using a 3.5mm (US size E/4) crochet hook and Cascade Ultra Pima.

ABBREVIATIONS

See page 127.

SPECIAL ABBREVIATION

MP (make picot): ch2, sl st in second ch from hook

Cushion cover front

(make 1)
Using 5mm (US size H/8) hook and A, ch71.
Row 1: 1dc in second ch from hook, 1dc in each ch to end, turn. *70 sts*.
Row 2: Ch1 (does not count as st), 1dc in each st to end, turn.
Rep Row 2 until work measures 40cm (16in).

BORDER

Round 1: Work a second dc in last st of prev row (corner made), work 1dc in each row end down left-hand side, 2dc in corner st, work 1dc in each st along bottom edge, 2dc in corner st, work 1dc in each row end up right-hand side, 2dc in corner st, sl st in first st of last row of cushion to join.
Fasten off.

Cushion cover upper back

(make 1)
Using 5mm (US size H/8) hook and A, ch71.
Row 1: 1dc in second ch from hook, 1dc in each ch to end, turn. *70 sts*.
Row 2: Ch1 (does not count as st), 1dc in each st to end, turn.
Rep Row 2 until work measures 25cm (10in).

BORDER

Round 1: Work a second dc in last st of prev row (corner made), work 1dc in each row end down left-hand side, 2dc in corner st, work 1dc in each st along bottom edge, 2dc in corner st, work 1dc in each row end up right-hand side, 2dc in corner st, sl st in first st of last row of cushion to join.
Fasten off.

Cushion cover lower back

(make 1)
Using 5mm (US size H/8) hook and A, ch71.
Row 1: 1dc in second ch from hook, 1 dc in each ch to end, turn. *70 sts.*
Row 2: Ch1 (does not count as st), 1dc in each st to end, turn.
Rep Row 2 until work measures 23.5cm (9¼in).

BORDER
Round 1: Work a second dc in last st of prev row (corner made), work 1dc in each row end down left-hand side, 2dc in corner st, work 1dc in each st along bottom edge, 2dc in corner st, work 1dc in each row end up right-hand side, 2dc in corner st, sl st in first st of last row of cushion to join.
Fasten off.

Mistletoe sprigs

(make 10)
Using 3.5mm (US size E/4) hook and B, ch11.
Leaf 1: Sl st in second ch from hook, sl st in each of next 3 ch, 1dc in each of next 4 ch, 1htr in next ch, 2htr in last ch, working down opposite side of ch, 1htr in each of next 4 ch, 1dc in each of next 3 ch, sl st in each of last 2 ch.
Stalk: Ch8, sl st in second ch from hook, sl st back to base of Leaf 1.
Leaf 2: Ch9, 1htr in second ch from hook, 1htr in each of next 2 ch, 1dc in each of next 3 ch, sl st in each of last 2 ch, working down opposite side of ch, sl st in each of next 3 ch, 1dc in each of next 3 ch, sl st in next ch, sl st in top of first st to join.
Fasten off.

Holly leaves (make 10)

Using 3.5mm (US size E/4) hook and C, ch12.
Round 1: 1dc in second ch from hook, 1dc in next ch, 1htr in each of next 2 ch, 1tr in each of next 2 ch, 1htr in each of next 3 ch, 1dc in each of last 2 ch, working down opposite side of ch, 1dc in each of next 3 ch, 1htr in next 2 ch, 1tr in each of next 2 ch, 1htr in each of next 2 ch, 1dc in last ch. *21 sts.*
Stalk: Ch6, sl st in second ch from hook, sl st in each ch back to base of leaf.
Round 2: Sl st in first st, MP, sl st in next st, [1dc in next st, MP, sl st in next st] 4 times, (1dc in next st, ch3, sl st in third ch from hook, sl st) in next st, working down opposite side of leaf, sl st in next st, [MP, sl st in next st, 1dc in next st] 4 times, sl st in next st, sl st in base of leaf to join.
Fasten off.

Holly berries

(make 14)
Using 2.5mm (US size B/1–C/2) hook and D, make a magic ring.
Round 1: 4dc in ring. *4 sts.*
Round 2: [1dc in next st, 2dc in next st] twice, sl st in first dc to join. *6 sts.*
Fasten off leaving a long yarn tail.
Use the yarn tail to close each holly berry at the back by running a gathering thread around the base and pulling it up tightly.

Making up and finishing

Sew in ends on the cushion cover. Lay the cushion cover front on a flat surface, RS down. Place the cushion cover upper back and lower back on top of the front piece so that the two back edges overlap, with RS up. Pin across the join at the back of the cushion where the opening will be. Pin the pompom edging all the way around the cushion edges, making sure that the front and back pieces are all joined. Using a sewing needle and thread stitch the sides together all the way around the cushion.

Turn the cushion over so that the RS is facing you and place the cushion pad inside the cover. Position the leaves where you want them to be for the wreath and hold in place with safety pins. Slide the cushion pad out. Slide a piece of cardboard inside to avoid the front and back of the cushion getting stitched together.

Using a sewing needle and thread stitch the leaves securely in place. Stitch the holly berries in place. Stitch the red velvet bow in place at the top of the wreath. Using a yarn needle threaded with E, work two or three French knots for mistletoe berries where the two leaves of each mistletoe sprig join.

Remove the cardboard and insert the cushion pad. Stitch the three snap fasteners into place so that the opening of the cushion is closed, and the fasteners are hidden underneath the overlapping flap. Using a sewing needle and thread, sew the three buttons onto the back of the cushion, directly above where the fasteners are.

NORDIC CHRISTMAS WREATH

Sometimes the simplest of designs is all that is needed and that's very much the case with this wreath. Just holly leaves and berries, a simple heart, and some red ribbon provide all the Christmassy feel you need!

SKILL LEVEL ●

YARN AND MATERIALS

Cascade Ultra Pima (100% cotton, 200m/219yd per 100g/3½oz ball) DK (light worsted) weight yarn:
  1 ball each of:
  Sprout shade 3740 (A)
  Wine shade 3713 (B)
  White shade 3728 (C)

Small amount of 100% polyester toy stuffing

1m (1yd) of 10mm (⅜in) wide red gingham ribbon

30cm (12in) twiggy wreath base

Short length of 5mm (¼in) wide red ribbon

25cm (10in) of 25mm (1in) wide red velvet ribbon

HOOKS AND EQUIPMENT

2.5mm (US size B/1–C/2) crochet hook

Yarn needle

Hot glue gun

FINISHED MEASUREMENTS

30cm (12in) diameter

TENSION (GAUGE)

One holly leaf measures approx. 6.5cm (2¼in) long, using 2.5mm (US size B/1–C/2) crochet hook and Cascade Ultra Pima.

ABBREVIATIONS

See page 127

SPECIAL ABBREVIATION

MP (make picot): ch2, sl st in second ch from hook

Holly berries

(make 17)
Using 2.5mm (US size B/1–C/2) hook and B, make a magic ring.
Round 1: 4dc in ring. *4 sts.*
Round 2: [1dc in next st, 2dc in next st) twice, sl st in first dc to join. *6 sts.*
Fasten off, leaving a long yarn tail.
Use the yarn tail to close each holly berry at the back by running a gathering thread around the base and pulling it up tightly.

Holly leaves

(make 14)
Using 2.5mm (US size B/1–C/2) hook and A, ch12.
Round 1: 1dc in second ch from hook, 1dc in each of next 2 ch, 1htr in each of next 2 ch, 1tr in each of next 2 ch, 1htr in each of next 2 ch, 1dc in next ch, (1dc, ch1, 1dc in last ch, working down opposite side of ch, 1dc in each of next 2 ch, 1htr in each of next 2 ch, 1tr in each of next 2 ch, 1htr in each of next 2 ch, 1dc in each of next 2 ch, sl st in first st to join.
Round 2: [(1dc, MP, 1dc) in next st, sl st in next st] 5 times, (sl st, ch3, sl st in third ch from hook, sl st) in next st, working down opposite side of leaf, [(1dc, MP, 1dc) in next st, sl st in next st] 5 times, MP, sl st in first st to join.
Fasten off.

Heart

(make 2)

Using 2.5mm (US size B/1–C/2) hook and B, ch2.

Row 1: 2dc in second ch from hook. *2 sts.*

Turn at end of this and every foll row.

Row 2: Ch1, 1dc in first st, 2dc in next st. *3 sts.*

Row 3: Ch1, 2dc in first st, 1dc in next st, 2dc in next st. *5 sts.*

Rows 4–6: Ch1, 2dc in first st, 1dc in each st to last st, 2dc in last st. *11 sts.*

Row 7: Ch1, 1dc in each st to end.

Rows 8–10: Ch1, 2dc in first st, 1dc in each st to last st, 2dc in last st. *17 sts.*

Rows 11–12: Ch1, 1dc in each st to end.

LOBE

Row 13: Ch1, 1dc in each of first 8 sts, turn.

Row 14: Ch1, 1dc in each of next 8 sts, turn.

Row 15: Dc2tog, 1dc in each of next 4 sts, dc2tog, turn. *6 sts.*

Row 16: Ch1, dc2tog, 1dc in each of next 2 sts, dc2tog, turn. *4 sts.*

Row 17: Ch1, [dc2tog] twice. *2 sts.*

Fasten off.

Rejoin yarn at other end of Row 13 and rep Rows 13–17 for second lobe.

Using B, work dc evenly around edge of heart, working a couple of extra dc around lobes to keep shape if needed.

Fasten off.

Making up and finishing

Sew in ends of all pieces. Tie one end of the 10mm (⅜in) gingham ribbon to the back of the wreath base and wrap the ribbon all the way around the wreath following the photograph as a guide, so that you have seven spaces in total between each ribbon wrap. Tie the ribbon securely at the back to finish.

Using the hot glue gun, stick two holly leaves and two or three berries into each space on the wreath.

Using a yarn needle threaded with C, embroider a simple Nordic design onto one of the heart pieces, following the photo as a guide. Using a yarn needle threaded with C, place the two hearts WS together and join by sewing blanket stitch all the way around the edge. Before finishing the seam, stuff slightly, then close the heart and fasten off. Sew in any ends. Thread the 5mm (¼in) red ribbon through the top of the heart and tie it to the wreath at the centre top.

Use the velvet ribbon to make a hanging loop at the back of the wreath.

NORDIC CHRISTMAS STOCKING STRING

This garland works brilliantly as an alternative Advent calendar, because both the stockings and the buckets can have little treats tucked away inside them. Once made, this garland can be brought out every year with the rest of your favourite festive decorations.

SKILL LEVEL ● ●

YARN AND MATERIALS

Cascade Ultra Pima (100% cotton, 200m/219yd per 100g/3½oz ball) DK (light worsted) weight yarn:
  1 ball each of:
  Wine shade 3713 (A)
  Light Grey shade 3808 (B)
  White shade 3728 (C)

Yarn and Colors Must-Have Minis (100% cotton, 25m/27yd per 10g/⅓oz ball) 4-ply (fingering) weight yarn:
  1 ball of White shade 001 (D)

Florist's wire for bucket handles

Card to line buckets

Approx. 1m (1yd) of 10mm (⅜in) wide red gingham ribbon

120cm (47in) of white cord

HOOKS AND EQUIPMENT

3.5mm (US size E/4) crochet hook

2.5mm (US size B/1–C/2) crochet hook

Locking stitch marker

Yarn needle

Sewing needle and thread

FINISHED MEASUREMENTS

Garland: length 90cm (35½in)

Bucket: height 5cm (2in), top diameter 5.5cm (2¼in)

Stocking: approx. length 10cm (4in)

TENSION (GAUGE)

15 sts x 15 rows = 6.5 x 7.5cm (2½ x 3in) working double crochet, using a 3.5mm (US size E/4) crochet hook and Cascade Ultra Pima.

ABBREVIATIONS

See page 127.

Stocking

(make 2 in A and B, 2 in A and C)
Using 3.5mm (US size E/4) hook and A, make a magic ring.
Round 1: 6dc in ring. *6 sts.*
Work in a continuous spiral. PM in last st and move up as each round is finished.
Round 2: 2dc in each st to end. *12 sts.*
Round 3: [1dc in next st, 2dc in next st] 6 times. *18 sts.*
Rounds 4–11: 1dc in each st to end.
Round 12: 1dc in each st to end, working last yrh in either B or C.
Row 13: Using B or C, 1dc in each of first 12 sts, turn.
Rows 14–16: Ch1 (does not count as st), 1dc in each of next 12 sts, turn. *12 sts.*
Fold foot flat, with second colour panel at heel. Working so seam will be on inside of stocking, join back of heel with a dc seam across the first 5 sts (working into corresponding sts from both sides of heel), work a sl st to join final pair of heel sts, completing the heel seam.
Fasten off B or C.

Round 17: Using A, work 15 dc evenly around opening of foot. *15 sts.*

Round 18: Work 1dc in each st to end, working 2dc in each of 2 centre back sts above heel seam. *17 sts.*

Rounds 19–25: 1dc in each st to end.

Round 26: 1dc in each st to end, working last yrh in either B or C.

Fasten off A.

Rounds 27–28: Using B or C, 1dc in each st to end.

Round 29: 2dc in first st, 1dc in each of next 9 sts, 2dc in next st, 1dc in each of next 6 sts. *19 sts.*

Rounds 30 and 31: 1dc in each st to end, sl st in top of first dc to join at end of last round.

Fasten off.

Bucket

(make 3)

BASE

Using 3.5mm (US size E/4) hook and B, make a magic ring.

Round 1: 6dc in ring. *6 sts.*

Work in a continuous spiral. PM in last st and move up as each round is finished.

Round 2: 2dc in each st to end. *12 sts.*

Round 3: [1dc in next st, 2dc in next st] 6 times. *18 sts.*

Round 4: 1dc in next st, 2dc in next st, [1dc in each of next 2 sts, 2dc in next st] 5 times, 1dc in last st. *24 sts.*

Round 5: [1dc in each of next 3 sts, 2dc in next st] 6 times, sl st in top of first dc to join round. *30 sts.*

SIDES

Beg working in rounds.

Round 6: Ch1 (does not count as st throughout), working in back loop only of each st, 1dc in each st to end, sl st in top of ch-1 to join. *30 sts.*

Round 7: Ch1, working in both loops, 1dc in next dc, 1dc in each st to end, sl st in top of ch-1 to join.

Round 8: Ch1, 1dc in each of next 14 dc, 2dc in next st, 1dc in each of next 14 sts, 2dc in next st, sl st in top of ch-1 to join. *32 sts.*

Rounds 9 and 10: Ch1, 1dc in next dc, 1dc in each st to end, sl st in top of ch-1 to join. *32 sts.*

Round 11: Ch1, 1dc in each of next 7 dc, 2dc in next st, 1dc in each of next 15 sts, 2dc in next st, 1dc in each of next 8 sts, sl st in top of ch-1 to join. *34 sts.*

Rounds 12–14: Ch1, 1dc in next dc, 1dc in each st to end, sl st in top of ch-1 to join.

Round 15: Ch1, 1dc in each of next 2 dc, 2dc in next st, 1dc in each of next 16 sts, 2dc in next st, 1dc in each of next 14 sts, sl st in top of ch-1 to join. *36 sts.*

Rounds 16–17: Ch1, 1dc in next dc, 1dc in each st to end, sl st in top of ch-1 to join.

Round 18: Ch1, sl st loosely in each st to end, sl st in top of ch-1 to join.

Fasten off.

Star

(make 3)

Using 2.5mm (US size B/1–C/2) hook and D, make a magic ring.

Round 1: 5dc in ring. *5 sts.*

Round 2: [2dc in next st] 5 times, sl st in top of first dc to join. *10 sts.*

Round 3: *Ch4, sl st in second ch from hook, 1dc in next ch, 1htr in next ch, miss next st of central circle, sl st in next st of central circle; rep from * 4 times to make 5 points in total, sl st in base of first point to join.

Fasten off.

Making up and finishing

Sew in all ends.

Using a needle and thread sew a star onto each bucket. Make a wire handle for each bucket and stitch each side in place. Line the bucket with card to give the sides rigidity. Cut 3 short lengths of gingham ribbon and tie in a bow around centre top of each handle.

Using a yarn needle threaded with D, decorate each stocking with straight stitches and French knots (see page 124), following the photograph as a guide. Fold down the top of the stocking and secure with a couple of small stitches. Cut 4 short lengths of gingham ribbon and stitch a small ribbon loop into the centre back of each stocking.

Lay the white cord out on a table and hang the stockings and buckets where you want them to be. Add a couple of stitches with the needle and thread to hold each item in place.

Tie loop knots at each end of the cord and add a bow of gingham ribbon at each end.

CHRISTMAS PLACE SETTINGS

For something a little different, why not make all of your Christmas dinner guests a mini festive wreath? They are very quick to complete and can be personalised with individual name tags.

SKILL LEVEL ●

YARN AND MATERIALS

For eight mini wreaths:
DMC Natura XL (100% cotton, 75m/82yd per 100g/3½oz ball) super chunky (super bulky) weight yarn:
  1 ball of shade 85 (A)

Cascade Ultra Pima Fine (100% cotton, 125m/137yd per 50g/1¾oz ball) 5-ply (sport) weight yarn:
  1 ball each of:
  Sprout shade 3740 (B)
  Wine shade 3713 (C)

8 wooden rings, 70mm (2¾in) diameter

8 gold craft jingle bells, 20mm (⅞in) size

8 small cardboard name tags

Approx. 1m (1yd) of 10mm (⅜in) wide red gingham ribbon

HOOKS AND EQUIPMENT

6mm (US size J/10) crochet hook

2mm (US size 0) crochet hook

Yarn needle

Hot glue gun

FINISHED MEASUREMENTS

8cm (3¼in) diameter

TENSION (GAUGE)

5 sts x 5 rows = 4 x 5cm (1½ x 2in) working double crochet, using a 6mm (US size J/10) crochet hook and DMC Natura XL.

15 sts x 15 rows = 5.5 x 6cm (2¼ x 2⅜in) working double crochet, using a 2mm (US size 0) crochet hook and Cascade Ultra Pima Fine.

ABBREVIATIONS

See page 127.

SPECIAL ABBREVIATION

MP (make picot): ch2, sl st in second ch from hook

Wreath

Attach A to the wooden ring with a knot.
Using 6mm (US size J/10) hook, work dc all around the ring, sl st in top of first dc to join.
Fasten off, leaving a long yarn tail.

Holly leaf

(make 16)
Using 2mm (US size 0) hook and B, ch6.
Sl st in second ch from hook, [MP, sl st in next st] 3 times, sl st in next st, MP (tip made), working down opposite side of ch, sl st in next st, [MP, sl st in next st] twice, sl st in next st.
Fasten off.

Making up and finishing

Using a yarn needle threaded with C, work two or three French knots (see page 124) at the base of each leaf for the berries.

Thread a bell onto the long yarn tail left at the end of the wreath, and then sew in the yarn tail to secure at the back of the wreath.

Fasten off.

Use a hot glue gun to stick 2 holly leaves at the base of each wreath. Make small bows in gingham ribbon and glue at the top of each wreath. Tie on a name tag.

TECHNIQUES

In this section, we explain how to master the simple crochet and finishing techniques that you need to make the projects in this book.

Holding the hook

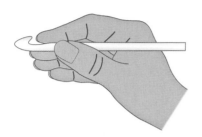

Pick up your hook as though you are picking up a pen or pencil. Keeping the hook held loosely between your fingers and thumb, turn your hand so that the palm is facing up and the hook is balanced in your hand and resting in the space between your index finger and your thumb.

You can also hold the hook like a knife – this may be easier if you are working with a large hook or with chunky yarn. Choose the method that you find most comfortable.

Holding the yarn

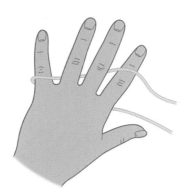

1 Pick up the yarn with your little finger in the opposite hand to your hook, with your palm facing upward and with the short end in front. Turn your hand to face downward, with the yarn on top of your index finger and under the other two fingers and wrapped right around the little finger, as shown above.

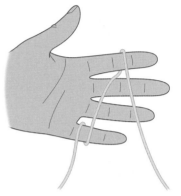

2 Turn your hand to face you, ready to hold the work in your middle finger and thumb. Keeping your index finger only at a slight curve, hold the work or the slip knot using the same hand, between your middle finger and your thumb and just below the crochet hook and loop/loops on the hook.

Making a slip knot

The simplest way is to make a circle with the yarn, so that the loop is facing downward.

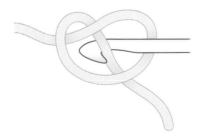

1 In one hand hold the circle at the top where the yarn crosses, and let the tail drop down at the back so that it falls across the centre of the loop. With your free hand or the tip of a crochet hook, pull a loop through the circle.

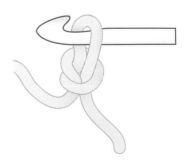

2 Put the hook into the loop and pull gently so that it forms a loose loop on the hook.

Yarn round hook (yrh)

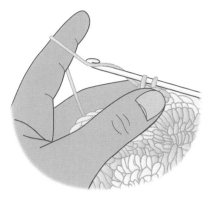

To create a stitch, catch the yarn from behind with the hook pointing upward. As you gently pull the yarn through the loop on the hook, turn the hook so it faces downward and slide the yarn through the loop. The loop on the hook should be kept loose enough for the hook to slide through easily.

Magic ring

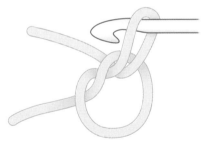

This is a useful starting technique if you do not want a visible hole in the centre of your round. Loop the yarn around your finger, insert the hook through the ring, yarn round hook, pull through the ring to make the first chain. Work the number of stitches required into the ring and then pull the end to tighten the centre ring and close the hole.

Chain (ch)

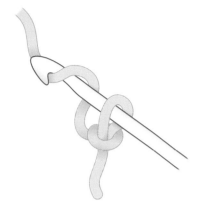

1 Using the hook, wrap the yarn round the hook ready to pull it through the loop on the hook.

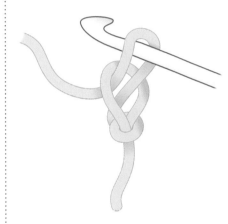

2 Pull through, creating a new loop on the hook. Continue in this way to create a chain of the required length.

Chain ring

If you are crocheting a round shape, one way of starting off is by crocheting a number of chains following the instructions in your pattern, and then joining them into a circle.

1 To join the chain into a circle, insert the crochet hook into the first chain that you made (not into the slip knot), yarn round hook.

2 Pull the yarn through the chain and through the loop on your hook at the same time, thereby creating a slip stitch and forming a circle. You now have a chain ring ready to work stitches into as instructed in the pattern.

Chain space (ch sp)

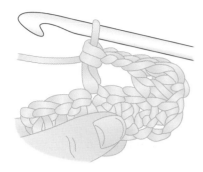

1 A chain space is the space that has been made under a chain in the previous round or row, and falls in between other stitches.

2 Stitches into a chain space are made directly into the hole created under the chain and not into the chain stitches themselves.

Slip stitch (sl st)

A slip stitch doesn't create any height and is often used as the last stitch to create a smooth and even round or row.

1 To make a slip stitch: first put the hook through the work, yarn round hook.

2 Pull the yarn through both the work and through the loop on the hook at the same time, so you will have 1 loop on the hook.

Making rounds

When working in rounds the work is not turned, so you are always working from one side. Depending on the pattern you are working, a 'round' can be square. Start each round by making one or more chains to create the height you need for the stitch you are working:
Double crochet = 1 chain
Half treble crochet = 2 chains
Treble crochet = 3 chains
Double treble = 4 chains
Work the required stitches to complete the round. At the end of the round, slip stitch into the top of the chain to close the round.

If you work in a spiral you do not need a turning chain. After completing the base ring, place a stitch marker in the first stitch and then continue to crochet around. When you have made a round and reached the point where the stitch marker is, work this stitch, take out the stitch marker from the previous round and put it back into the first stitch of the new round. A safety pin or piece of yarn in a contrasting colour makes a good stitch marker.

Making rows

When making straight rows you turn the work at the end of each row and make a turning chain to create the height you need for the stitch you are working with, as for making rounds.
Double crochet = 1 chain
Half treble crochet = 2 chains
Treble crochet = 3 chains
Double treble = 4 chains

Working into top of stitch

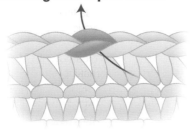

Unless otherwise directed, always insert the hook under both of the two loops on top of the stitch – this is the standard technique.

Working into front loop of stitch (FLO)

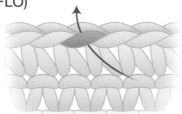

To work into the front loop of a stitch, pick up the front loop from underneath at the front of the work.

Working into back loop of stitch (BLO)

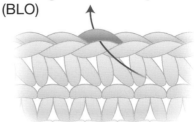

To work into the back loop of the stitch, insert the hook between the front and the back loop, picking up the back loop from the front of the work.

How to measure a tension (gauge) square

Using the hook and the yarn recommended in the pattern, make a number of chains to measure approximately 15cm (6in). Working in the stitch pattern given for the tension measurements, work enough rows to form a square. Fasten off.

Take a ruler, place it horizontally across the square and, using pins, mark a 10cm (4in) area. Repeat vertically to form a 10cm (4in) square on the fabric.

Count the number of stitches across, and the number of rows within the square, and compare against the tension given in the pattern.

If your numbers match the pattern then use this size hook and yarn for your project. If you have more stitches, then your tension is tighter than recommended and you need to use a larger hook. If you have fewer stitches, then your tension is looser and you will need a smaller hook.

Make tension squares using different size hooks until you have matched the tension in the pattern, and use this hook to make the project.

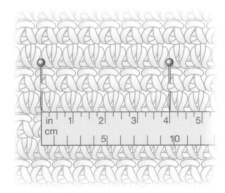

Double crochet (dc)

1 Insert the hook into your work, yarn round hook and pull the yarn through the work only. You will then have 2 loops on the hook.

2 Yarn round hook again and pull through the two loops on the hook. You will be left with 1 loop on the hook.

Half treble crochet (htr)

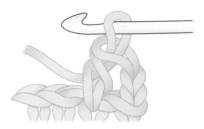

1 Before inserting the hook into the work, wrap the yarn round the hook and put the hook through the work with the yarn wrapped around.

2 Yarn round hook again and pull through the first loop on the hook. You now have 3 loops on the hook.

3 Yarn round hook and pull the yarn through all 3 loops. You will be left with 1 loop on the hook.

Treble crochet (tr)

1 Before inserting the hook into the work, wrap the yarn round the hook. Put the hook through the work with the yarn wrapped around, yarn round hook again and pull through the first loop on the hook. You now have 3 loops on the hook.

2 Yarn round hook again, pull the yarn through the first 2 loops on the hook. You now have 2 loops on the hook.

3 Pull the yarn through 2 loops again. You will be left with 1 loop on the hook.

Double treble (dtr)

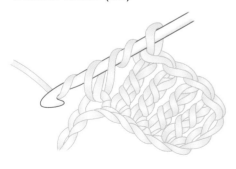

Yarn round hook twice, insert the hook into the stitch, yarn round hook, pull a loop through (4 loops on hook), yarn round hook, pull the yarn through 2 stitches (3 loops on hook), yarn round hook, pull a loop through the next 2 stitches (2 loops on hook), yarn round hook, pull a loop through the last 2 stitches. You will be left with 1 loop on the hook.

Front post treble (FPtr)

Raised stitches are created by making stitches around the 'posts' – or 'stems' – of the stitches in the previous row/round. Here the stitches are being worked around to the front.

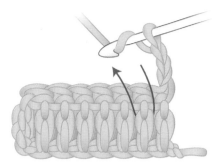

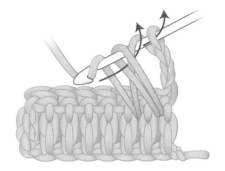

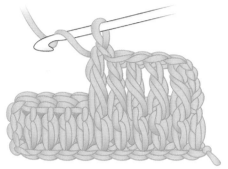

1 Yarn round hook and insert the hook from the front and around the post (the stem) of the next treble from right to left.

2 Yarn round hook and pull the yarn through the work, yarn round hook and pull the yarn through the first 2 loops on the hook.

3 Yarn round hook and pull the yarn through the 2 loops on the hook (1 loop on the hook).

Bobble

Bobbles are created when working on wrong-side rows and the bobble is then pushed out towards the right-side row. This is a four-treble cluster bobble (4trCL).

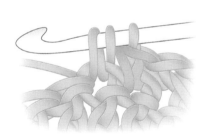

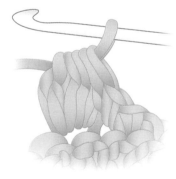

1 Yarn round hook and then insert the hook in the stitch, yarn round hook and pull the yarn through the work.

2 Yarn round hook and pull the yarn through the first 2 loops on the hook (2 loops on hook).

3 Repeat steps 1 and 2 three more times in the same stitch, yarn round hook and pull through all 5 loops on the hook.

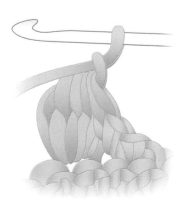

4 You can also make 1 chain to complete the bobble.

Picots

A picot is a little bobble texture that is often used to create decorative little points along the outer edge of an edging. This sample shows how to make a 3ch-picot, but follow the instructions in the pattern for the number of chains to make.

1 Make 14ch.
Row 1: 1dc in second ch from hook, 1dc in each ch to end.
Row 2: 1ch, 1dc in each of next 2 sts, 3tr in next st, *1dc in each of the next 3 sts, 3tr in next st: rep from * twice more, 2dc in each of last 2 sts.
Row 3 (picot row): 1ch, 1dc in each of next 2 dc, 1dc in top of next tr, *3ch.

2 Ss in third ch from hook (one picot made).
1dc in top of next tr.

3 Rep from * once more, 3ch, ss in third ch from hook (picot made)**, 1dc in each of next 3 dc, 1dc in top of next tr; rep from * ending last rep at **, 1dc in each of last two dc.

Increasing

Make two or three stitches into one stitch or space from the previous row. The illustration shows a treble crochet increase being made.

Decreasing

You can decrease by either missing the next stitch and continuing to crochet, or by crocheting two or more stitches together. The basic technique for crocheting stitches together is the same, no matter which stitch you are using.

DOUBLE CROCHET TWO STITCHES TOGETHER (dc2tog)

1 Insert the hook into your work, yarn round hook and pull the yarn through the work (2 loops on hook). Insert the hook in next stitch, yarn round hook and pull the yarn through.

2 Yarn round hook again and pull through all 3 loops on the hook. You will then have 1 loop on the hook.

Joining yarn at the end of a row or round

You can use this technique when changing colour, or when joining in a new ball of yarn as one runs out.

1 Keep the loop of the old yarn on the hook. Drop the tail and catch a loop of the strand of the new yarn with the crochet hook.

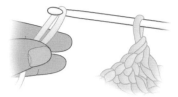

2 Draw the new yarn through the loop on the hook, keeping the old loop drawn tight and continue as instructed in the pattern.

Joining in new yarn after fastening off

1 Fasten off the old colour (see page 124). Make a slip knot with the new colour (see page 116). Insert the hook into the stitch at the beginning of the next row, then through the slip knot.

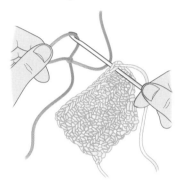

2 Draw the loop of the slip knot through to the front of the work. Carry on working using the new colour, following the instructions in the pattern.

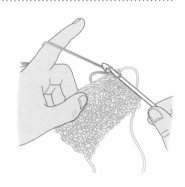

Joining yarn in the middle of a row or round

For a neat colour join in the middle of a row or round, use these methods.

JOINING A NEW COLOUR INTO DOUBLE CROCHET

1 Make a double crochet stitch (see page 119), but do not draw the final loop through, so there are 2 loops on the hook. Drop the old yarn, catch the new yarn with the hook and draw it through both loops to complete the stitch and join in the new colour at the same time.

2 Continue to crochet with the new yarn. Cut the old yarn leaving a 15cm (6in) tail and weave the tail in (see right) after working a row, or once the work is complete.

JOINING A NEW COLOUR INTO TREBLE CROCHET

1 Make a treble crochet stitch (see page 120), but do not draw the final loop through, so there are 2 loops on the hook. Drop the old yarn, catch the new yarn with the hook and draw it through both loops to complete the stitch and join in the new colour at the same time.

2 Continue to crochet with the new yarn. Cut the old yarn leaving a 15cm (6in) tail and weave the tail in (see page 124) after working a row, or once the work is complete.

Enclosing a yarn tail

You may find that the yarn tail gets in the way as you work; you can enclose this into the stitches as you go by placing the tail at the back as you wrap the yarn. This also saves having to sew this tail end in later.

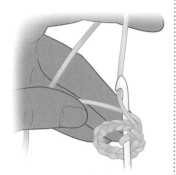

Fastening off

When you have finished crocheting, you need to fasten off the stitches to stop all your work unravelling.

Draw up the final loop of the last stitch to make it bigger. Cut the yarn, leaving a tail of approximately 10cm (4in) – unless a longer end is needed for sewing up. Pull the tail all the way through the loop and pull the loop up tightly.

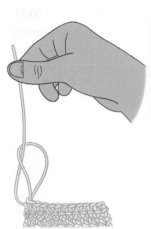

Weaving in yarn ends

It is important to weave in the tail ends of the yarn so that they are secure and your crochet won't unravel. Thread a yarn needle with the tail end of yarn. On the wrong side, take the needle through the crochet one stitch down on the edge, then take it through the stitches, working in a gentle zig-zag. Work through four or five stitches then return in the opposite direction. Remove the needle, pull the crochet gently to stretch it and trim the end.

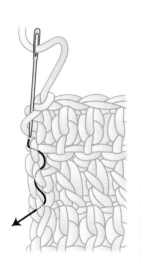

Making a French knot

Bring the needle up from the back of the fabric to the front. Wrap the thread two or three times around the tip of the needle, then reinsert the needle at the point where it first emerged, holding the wrapped threads with the thumbnail of your non-stitching hand, and pull the needle all the way through. The wraps will form a knot on the surface of the fabric.

Blocking

Crochet can tend to curl, so to make flat pieces stay flat you may need to block them. Pin the piece out to the correct size and shape on an ironing board, then cover with a cloth and press or steam gently (depending on the type of yarn) and allow to dry completely before unpinning and removing from the board.

When making small items to be attached to wreaths or garlands, you will find that taking the time to block and stiffen the pieces will make a huge difference to the finished effect. Without either of these processes you will find that small pieces in particular will curl out of shape and lose their definition. You'll need blocking pins, some soft foam mats (such as the ones sold as children's play mats) and some ironing spray starch. Pin each item out to shape and size on the mats and then spray with the starch. Allow to dry for a day before attaching the elements to your make.

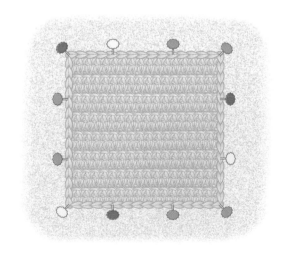

Making an oversewn seam

An oversewn join gives a nice flat seam and is the simplest and most common joining technique.

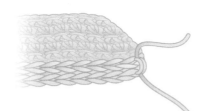

1 Thread a yarn sewing needle with the yarn you're using in the project. Place the pieces to be joined with right sides together.

2 Insert the needle in one corner in the top loops of the stitches of both pieces and pull up the yarn, leaving a tail of about 5cm (2in). Go into the same place with the needle and pull up the yarn again; repeat two or three times to secure the yarn at the start of the seam.

3 Join the pieces together by taking the needle through the loops at the top of corresponding stitches on each piece to the end. Fasten off the yarn at the end, as in step 2.

Making a double crochet seam

With a double crochet seam you join two pieces together using a crochet hook and working a double crochet stitch through both pieces, instead of sewing them together with a tail of yarn and a yarn sewing needle. This makes a quick and strong seam and gives a slightly raised finish to the edging. For a less raised seam, follow the same basic technique, but work each stitch in slip stitch rather than double crochet.

1 Start by lining up the two pieces with wrong sides together. Insert the hook in the top 2 loops of the stitch of the first piece, then into the corresponding stitch on the second piece.

2 Complete the double crochet stitch as normal and continue on the next stitches as directed in the pattern. This gives a raised effect if the double crochet stitches are made on the right side of the work.

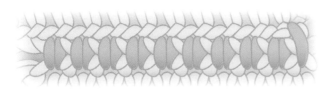

3 You can work with the wrong side of the work facing (with the pieces right side facing) if you don't want this effect and it still creates a good strong join.

Surface crochet

Surface crochet is a simple way to add extra decoration to a finished item, working slip stitches over the surface of the fabric.

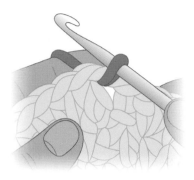 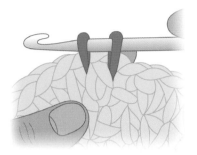 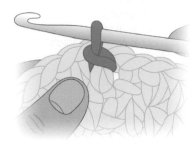

1 Using a contrast yarn, make a slip knot (see page 116). Holding the yarn with the slip knot behind the work and the hook in front, insert the hook between two stitches from front to the back and catch the slip knot behind the work with the hook. Draw the slip knot back through, so there is 1 loop on the hook at the front of the work.

2 Insert the hook between the next 2 stitches, yarn round hook and draw a loop through to the front. You will now have 2 loops on the hook.

3 Pull the first loop on the hook through the second loop to complete the first slip stitch on the surface of the work. Repeat steps 2 and 3 to make the next slip stitch. To join two ends with an invisible join, cut the yarn and thread onto a yarn needle. Insert the needle up through the last stitch, into the first stitch as if you were crocheting it, then into the back loop of the previous stitch. Fasten off on the wrong side.

CROCHET STITCH CONVERSION CHART

Crochet stitches are worked in the same way in both the UK and the USA, but the stitch names are not the same and identical names are used for different stitches. Below is a list of the UK terms used in this book, and the equivalent US terms.

UK TERM	US TERM
double crochet (dc)	single crochet (sc)
half treble (htr)	half double crochet (hdc)
treble (tr)	double crochet (dc)
double treble (dtr)	treble (tr)
triple treble (ttr)	double treble (dtr)
quadruple treble (qtr)	triple treble (ttr)
tension	gauge
yarn round hook (yrh)	yarn over hook (yoh)

ABBREVIATIONS

approx.	approximately
beg	beginning
BLO	back loop(s) only
ch	chain
ch sp	chain space
cm	centimetre(s)
cont	continu(e)ing
dc	double crochet
dc2tog	double crochet 2 stitches together
dec	decreas(e)ing
dtr	double treble
FLO	front loop only
foll	follow(s)ing
FPtr	front post treble
g	gram(mes)
htr	half treble
in	inch(es)
inc	increas(e)ing
m	metre(s)
MB	make bobble
mm	millimetre(s)
MP	make picot
oz	ounce(s)
PM	place marker
rem	remaining
rep	repeat
RS	right side(s)
sl st	slip stitch
sp	space
st(s)	stitch(es)
tog	together
tr	treble
ttr	triple treble
yd	yard(s)
WS	wrong side(s)
yrh	yarn round hook
[ ]	work section between square brackets number of times stated
*	asterisk indicates beginning of repeated section of pattern

SUPPLIERS

For reasons of space we cannot cover all stockists, so please explore the local yarn shops and online stores in your own country.

UK

lovecrafts
Online sales
www.lovecrafts.com

Wool
Yarn, hooks
Store in Bath.
+44 (0)1225 469144
www.woolbath.co.uk

Susie Watson Designs
Pompom trims
susiewatsondesigns.co.uk

Deramores
Online sales
www.deramores.com

Hobbycraft
Craft supplies including wreath bases.
www.hobbycraft.co.uk

Laughing Hens
Online sales
Tel: +44 (0) 1829 740903
www.laughinghens.com

John Lewis
Yarns and craft supplies
Telephone numbers of stores on website
www.johnlewis.com

USA

Knitting Fever Inc.
www.knittingfever.com

WEBS
www.yarn.com

Jo-Ann Fabric and Craft Stores
Yarns and craft supplies www.joann.com

Michaels
Craft supplies
www.michaels.com

AUSTRALIA

Black Sheep Wool 'n' Wares
Retail store and online
Tel: +61 (0)2 6779 1196
www.blacksheepwool.com.au

Sun Spun
Retail store only (Canterbury, Victoria)
Tel: +61 (0)3 9830 1609

YARN COMPANIES

Cascade
Stockist locator on website
www.cascadeyarns.com

DMC
Stockist locator on website
www.dmc.com

Rowan Yarns
Stockist locator on website www. knitrowan.com

If you wish to substitute a different yarn for the one recommended in the pattern, try the **Yarnsub** website for suggestions: www.yarnsub.com

ACKNOWLEDGEMENTS

There are many 'thank yous' I would like to say now that this book is finished and ready to go out in to the world. It would not have seen the light of day without the incredible team behind me, making the creation of my second book just as amazing an experience as the first.

First, to everyone at CICO Books who have made the dream a reality – thank you. I am so thankful for having had such a hard-working team behind this book who have taken me through each stage with such care and attention. I could not have wished for anything better and the finished result, with all the beautiful photographs and styling, simply takes my breath away.

An enormous thank you also to my friends at lovecrafts.com who provided every centimetre of yarn used to create each project in this book. They have supported me right from the very start of my crochet designing journey and I am so enormously grateful to have them behind me.

Finally, to my family – thank you! Thanks for every tiny bit of encouragement, the suggestions and ideas when my mind went blank, the endless cups of tea, the meals on the table, and for having such total faith in me, believing that I could do it.

There are not enough words – thank you Dave, Meg, Beth and Immi.

INDEX

crocheted home